United Nations: Celebrating Successes and Imperfections

ROBERTO MIGUEL RODRIGUEZ

2023

Copyright Page

TITLE: United Nations: Celebrating Successes and Imperfections

1ST Edition

Copyright @ 2023

ISBN: 9798223399834

Table of Contents

United Nations: Celebrating Successes and Imperfections

By Roberto Miguel Rodriguez

Chapter 1: United Nations: The Successes of an Imperfect Organization

The Formation of the United Nations

The formation of the United Nations (UN) marked a significant turning point in international relations. Born out of the ashes of the devastating Second World War, the UN emerged as a beacon of hope for a world desperate to prevent another global conflict. This chapter delves into the origins and creation of the UN, highlighting its mission and the challenges it faced in its early years.

In the aftermath of World War II, the world recognized the need for a new international organization that would promote peace, security, and cooperation among nations. The United Nations was officially established on October 24, 1945, with the signing of the UN Charter by 51 founding member states. The Charter provided a framework for the organization's goals and principles, emphasizing the importance of international law, human rights, and the peaceful settlement of disputes.

The UN's formation was a monumental achievement, bringing together countries from diverse backgrounds and ideologies. Its structure, consisting of the General Assembly, Security Council, Secretariat, and specialized agencies, was designed to ensure collective decision-making and representation of all member states.

One of the UN's primary objectives was to maintain international peace and security. The Security Council, with its five permanent members and ten rotating members, was entrusted with this responsibility. However, the dynamics of the Cold War era often hindered its effectiveness, as the veto power of the permanent members led to gridlock on critical issues.

Nevertheless, the UN has had numerous successes in its pursuit of peacekeeping missions. It has played a crucial role in resolving conflicts and preventing wars through diplomatic negotiations and peacekeeping operations. From Cyprus to Rwanda, the UN's peacekeeping efforts have made a tangible impact in stabilizing regions torn by violence and facilitating post-conflict reconstruction.

Beyond peacekeeping, the UN has been at the forefront of promoting gender equality, women's empowerment, and human rights. It has championed initiatives aimed at eliminating discrimination and violence against women, ensuring their equal participation in decision-making processes, and advancing their economic and social rights.

The UN has also been instrumental in addressing global health challenges. Through its specialized agencies such as the World Health Organization (WHO), it has led efforts to combat diseases, improve healthcare systems, and promote access to essential medicines worldwide. In recent years, the UN has been at the forefront of combating the COVID-19 pandemic, coordinating global responses and advocating for equitable vaccine distribution.

Additionally, the UN has been a driving force in addressing climate change and environmental sustainability. The landmark Paris Agreement, adopted in 2015, was a significant milestone in global efforts to reduce greenhouse gas emissions and mitigate the impacts of climate change. The UN's efforts in promoting sustainable development goals (SDGs), including renewable energy, sustainable cities, and responsible consumption and production, have been critical in building a more sustainable future.

The United Nations has also played a crucial role in promoting international cooperation and diplomacy. Through its platforms such as the General Assembly and various specialized agencies, the UN facilitates dialogue, negotiation, and collaboration among nations to address global challenges collectively.

In conclusion, the formation of the United Nations was a pivotal moment in history, signaling a commitment to international peace, cooperation, and justice. While it has faced numerous challenges and criticisms, the UN has undeniably made significant contributions in various areas, from peacekeeping missions to promoting gender equality, combating climate change, and fostering global development. As the world continues to evolve, the UN remains a vital institution, striving to address the imperfections that arise and celebrating the successes achieved in creating a better world for all.

The United Nations Charter: A Blueprint for Peace

The United Nations Charter stands as a testament to the world's commitment to peace and security. Adopted on June 26, 1945, it serves as the foundation for the work of the United Nations and has become a blueprint for peace for nations across the globe.

The Charter, with its 111 articles, outlines the principles and purposes of the United Nations, and it has played a vital role in preventing conflicts and promoting peaceful resolutions. It has provided a framework for nations to come together, discuss their differences, and find common ground in the pursuit of peace.

One of the most significant achievements of the United Nations Charter has been the establishment of United Nations peacekeeping missions. These missions have been instrumental in preventing and resolving conflicts, as well as promoting stability and security in war-torn regions. From the Congo to Cyprus, from Rwanda to Sierra Leone, United Nations peacekeepers have made a tangible impact on the ground, saving lives and facilitating the transition to peace.

The Charter has also been instrumental in promoting gender equality and women's empowerment. It recognizes the fundamental rights and dignity of women and calls for their equal participation in decision-making processes. Through various initiatives and programs, the United Nations has worked tirelessly to promote gender equality, combat violence against women, and ensure equal access to education and healthcare.

Moreover, the United Nations has played a pivotal role in addressing global health challenges. From eradicating smallpox to combating HIV/AIDS, the United Nations has spearheaded international efforts to improve public health and reduce disease burdens. By coordinating resources, sharing knowledge, and advocating for equitable access to healthcare, the United Nations has made significant strides in improving health outcomes worldwide.

The Charter has also been a driving force in combating climate change and promoting environmental sustainability. Through the adoption of the Paris Agreement and other initiatives, the United Nations has rallied nations to take collective action to mitigate the impacts of climate change and transition to a sustainable future.

Furthermore, the United Nations has been at the forefront of international development and poverty reduction efforts. Through programs such as the Millennium Development Goals and the Sustainable Development Goals, the United Nations has mobilized resources, fostered partnerships, and implemented strategies to alleviate poverty and improve the lives of the world's most vulnerable populations.

In addition to its contributions to peace, health, and development, the United Nations has been a staunch advocate for human rights and global justice. Through the Universal Declaration of Human Rights and various human rights conventions, the United Nations has set international standards and promoted respect for human rights worldwide.

The United Nations has also been actively involved in providing humanitarian aid and disaster relief. From responding to natural disasters to addressing humanitarian crises, the United Nations has played a critical role in providing lifesaving assistance and supporting the most vulnerable populations.

Through its initiatives in promoting education and literacy worldwide, the United Nations has helped millions of children gain access to quality education. By prioritizing education as a fundamental right, the United Nations has worked towards building a brighter and more inclusive future for all.

Moreover, the United Nations has been a key player in promoting international cooperation and diplomacy. Through its forums, such as the General Assembly and Security Council, the United Nations has provided a platform for nations to engage in dialogue, resolve conflicts, and build partnerships based on mutual understanding and respect.

Lastly, the United Nations has been instrumental in promoting sustainable development goals (SDGs). These goals, ranging from poverty eradication to climate action, serve as a roadmap for nations to achieve a more sustainable and equitable future.

In conclusion, the United Nations Charter has provided a blueprint for peace, serving as a guiding document for nations to come together, address global challenges, and build a better world. Despite its imperfections, the United Nations has achieved significant successes in various areas, from peacekeeping to promoting gender equality, from combating climate change to promoting international cooperation. As we celebrate these successes, we must also acknowledge the ongoing challenges and strive for a more perfect United Nations that can effectively address the ever-evolving global issues we face today.

The United Nations' Role in Maintaining International Security

The United Nations (UN) plays a crucial role in maintaining international security, ensuring peace, and preventing conflicts from escalating into devastating wars. With its diverse membership and global reach, the UN has become a vital platform for nations to address security challenges collectively. This subchapter explores the UN's multifaceted efforts in maintaining international security, from peacekeeping missions to promoting disarmament and non-proliferation.

One of the most notable successes of the UN in maintaining international security is its peacekeeping missions. Since its establishment, the UN has deployed peacekeepers to conflict zones around the world, helping to restore stability and protect vulnerable populations. These missions have been instrumental in preventing conflicts from escalating and facilitating peace negotiations. From Rwanda to Bosnia and Herzegovina, the UN's peacekeepers have made significant contributions to ending violence and fostering reconciliation.

In addition to peacekeeping, the UN has been actively engaged in promoting disarmament and non-proliferation of weapons of mass destruction. Through its specialized agencies such as the International Atomic Energy Agency (IAEA), the UN works to prevent the spread of nuclear weapons and ensure the peaceful use of nuclear energy. The UN's efforts in this field have led to landmark agreements, such as the Treaty on the Non-Proliferation of Nuclear Weapons (NPT), which has significantly reduced the number of nuclear weapons globally.

Moreover, the UN recognizes the critical link between security and development. It understands that sustainable development and poverty reduction are essential for long-term peace and stability. Thus, the UN actively promotes international development and poverty reduction through its various programs and initiatives. By addressing the root causes of conflicts, such as poverty, inequality, and lack of access to education and healthcare, the UN contributes to building peaceful and prosperous societies.

The UN's role in maintaining international security goes beyond traditional military interventions. It also includes addressing emerging security challenges, such as climate change, global health crises, and terrorism. The UN leads international efforts in combating climate change and environmental sustainability through conventions like the Paris Agreement. It also coordinates responses to global health challenges, as seen in its response to the Ebola outbreak in West Africa.

In conclusion, the UN's role in maintaining international security is multifaceted and indispensable. Through peacekeeping missions, disarmament efforts, and promoting sustainable development, the UN strives to prevent conflicts, protect vulnerable populations, and foster peace and stability. As the world faces unprecedented challenges, such as climate change and terrorism, the UN's role in maintaining international security will continue to evolve to address these emerging threats. By engaging diplomats, scholars, educators, journalists, politicians, and the public, this subchapter aims to shed light on the successes and imperfections of the UN's efforts in maintaining international security.

The United Nations' Efforts in Preventing and Resolving Conflicts

Conflicts and disputes have plagued humanity since time immemorial. However, in the aftermath of the devastating World War II, the international community recognized the urgent need for a global organization that could prevent conflicts and promote peaceful resolutions. Thus, the United Nations (UN) was born, with the primary objective of maintaining international peace and security. Over the years, the UN has made significant strides in preventing and resolving conflicts, showcasing its successes as well as acknowledging its imperfections.

One of the most notable achievements of the UN in conflict prevention and resolution is its peacekeeping missions. These missions have played a pivotal role in reducing violence, protecting civilians, and facilitating political transitions in war-torn countries. From the iconic mission in the Congo to the ongoing efforts in South Sudan, the UN peacekeepers have made a tangible impact on the ground, often at great personal risk. These missions have not only saved lives but also laid the foundation for sustainable peace and stability in conflict-affected regions.

Moreover, the UN has been at the forefront of promoting gender equality and women's empowerment as crucial components of conflict prevention and resolution. Through its resolutions and initiatives, the UN has successfully mainstreamed the inclusion of women in peace processes, ensuring their voices are heard and their rights protected. This recognition of women's agency in peacebuilding has led to more comprehensive and sustainable outcomes in conflict-affected areas.

In addition to conflict prevention, the UN has continuously addressed global health challenges, recognizing that health crises can exacerbate conflicts and hinder peacebuilding efforts. From combating HIV/AIDS to responding to the Ebola outbreak, the UN has played a critical role in coordinating international responses, mobilizing resources, and strengthening health systems to prevent the spread of diseases and save lives.

Furthermore, the UN has been a driving force in combating climate change and promoting environmental sustainability. Through initiatives such as the Paris Agreement, the UN has brought together nations to collectively address the existential threat of climate change. By mobilizing political will, promoting renewable energy, and fostering sustainable development practices, the UN is paving the way for a more sustainable and resilient future.

Overall, the United Nations' efforts in preventing and resolving conflicts have had a profound impact on global peace and security. From peacekeeping missions to promoting gender equality, from addressing health crises to combating climate change, the UN has consistently demonstrated its commitment to creating a better world. While challenges and imperfections exist, the UN remains an indispensable organization in promoting international cooperation, diplomacy, and sustainable development. It is through collective efforts that we can build a more peaceful, just, and sustainable world for future generations.

The United Nations' Peacekeeping Missions: Challenges and Achievements

Peacekeeping missions conducted by the United Nations have been instrumental in maintaining peace and stability in various regions of the world. These missions have faced numerous challenges but have also achieved commendable successes in their endeavors. This subchapter explores the challenges faced by the United Nations' peacekeeping missions and highlights their notable achievements.

One of the primary challenges faced by peacekeeping missions is the complexity of the conflicts they are deployed to. Conflicts often involve multiple parties with varying interests and deep-rooted grievances. This complexity requires peacekeepers to navigate through intricate political landscapes and find common ground for dialogue and negotiation. Moreover, peacekeepers often operate in volatile and dangerous environments, risking their lives to protect civilians and maintain peace.

Despite these challenges, United Nations peacekeeping missions have achieved significant successes. These missions have successfully mediated peace agreements, facilitated the disarmament and demobilization of combatants, and supported the establishment of democratic processes in post-conflict countries. For example, the United Nations Mission in Liberia (UNMIL) played a crucial role in ending the civil war and assisting with the country's transition to peace and democracy.

Another notable achievement of United Nations peacekeeping missions is their contribution to the protection and promotion of human rights, particularly in conflict-affected areas. Peacekeepers have been instrumental in preventing human rights abuses, including sexual violence, and ensuring the safe return of displaced persons. The United Nations Mission in South Sudan (UNMISS) has made significant progress in protecting civilians and supporting efforts to address sexual and gender-based violence in the country.

Additionally, United Nations peacekeeping missions have played a vital role in promoting international cooperation and diplomacy. Peacekeepers often work alongside regional organizations and other stakeholders to facilitate dialogue and foster peaceful resolutions. The United Nations Organization Stabilization Mission in the Democratic

Republic of the Congo (MONUSCO) has been actively involved in supporting regional efforts to address the root causes of conflict and promote stability in the Great Lakes region.

In conclusion, United Nations peacekeeping missions face numerous challenges in their pursuit of global peace and stability. However, their achievements in mediating conflicts, protecting human rights, and promoting international cooperation are commendable. By addressing these challenges and building on their successes, United Nations peacekeeping missions continue to play a crucial role in maintaining peace and supporting the aspirations of nations worldwide.

The United Nations' Efforts in Promoting Humanitarian Assistance

Humanitarian assistance is at the core of the United Nations' mission to alleviate human suffering and promote global peace and prosperity. Over the years, the UN has played a critical role in responding to humanitarian crises and providing aid to those in need. This subchapter explores the various ways in which the UN has dedicated its efforts to advance humanitarian assistance.

One of the key achievements of the United Nations in the realm of humanitarian aid is the establishment of the Office for the Coordination of Humanitarian Affairs (OCHA). OCHA serves as the focal point for coordinating humanitarian response efforts, ensuring effective and timely assistance in times of crisis. Through its coordination mechanisms, OCHA brings together governments, organizations, and other stakeholders to provide a unified response to emergencies, such as natural disasters, conflicts, and pandemics.

Furthermore, the UN has been instrumental in setting international standards and frameworks for humanitarian action. The Sphere Project, initiated by the UN, has developed a set of minimum standards for humanitarian response, encompassing areas such as water supply, sanitation, nutrition, and shelter. These standards serve as a guideline for humanitarian actors and ensure that assistance is provided in a principled, efficient, and accountable manner.

In addition to coordination and standards, the UN has facilitated financial support for humanitarian assistance through the Central Emergency Response Fund (CERF). CERF provides rapid and predictable funding to address urgent needs in sudden-onset emergencies and underfunded crises. This mechanism allows for a swift response to crises, enabling humanitarian organizations to save lives and alleviate suffering promptly.

The United Nations has also been actively engaged in promoting international norms and policies to protect and assist vulnerable populations during conflicts. The Guiding Principles on Internal Displacement, developed by the UN, provide a comprehensive framework for addressing the needs of internally displaced persons (IDPs). These principles emphasize the importance of protection, assistance, and durable solutions for IDPs, ensuring their rights and well-being are upheld.

Moreover, the UN has been at the forefront of advocating for the protection of civilians in armed conflicts. Through its peacekeeping missions, the UN works to safeguard the lives and rights of civilians affected by conflicts, while also providing vital assistance, such as food, water, and medical care. These efforts contribute to the overall stability and recovery of conflict-affected regions.

In conclusion, the United Nations' efforts in promoting humanitarian assistance have been instrumental in saving lives, alleviating suffering, and promoting resilience in times of crisis. Through coordination, setting standards, providing financial support, and advocating for the rights of vulnerable populations, the UN has made significant contributions to the field of humanitarian aid. However, challenges persist, and the UN continues to work towards improving its response mechanisms and ensuring that humanitarian assistance reaches those who need it most.

Chapter 2: United Nations Peacekeeping Missions and Their Impact

The History and Evolution of UN Peacekeeping

Introduction:

The United Nations (UN) is a remarkable organization that has played a pivotal role in maintaining peace and security around the world. One of its most important functions is peacekeeping, which involves the deployment of UN forces to conflict zones to prevent or resolve conflicts. This subchapter will explore the history and evolution of UN peacekeeping, highlighting its successes and imperfections.

Origins of UN Peacekeeping:

UN peacekeeping traces its origins back to the early years of the organization. Following the devastation of World War II, the UN Charter was adopted in 1945, with the primary goal of preventing future conflicts. The first UN peacekeeping mission, the UN Truce Supervision Organization (UNTSO), was established in 1948 to monitor the armistice between Israel and its Arab neighbors.

Evolution and Expansion:

Over the decades, UN peacekeeping has evolved and expanded in response to changing global dynamics. The end of the Cold War saw a significant increase in the number of peacekeeping missions, as the UN sought to address conflicts in various regions, including Africa, the Balkans, and the Middle East. The UN's efforts in promoting gender equality and women's empowerment have also been integrated into peacekeeping operations, recognizing the vital role that women play in conflict prevention and resolution.

Challenges and Criticisms:

Despite its successes, UN peacekeeping has faced several challenges and criticisms. One of the key criticisms is the lack of adequate resources and funding, which often hampers the effectiveness of peacekeeping missions. Additionally, peacekeepers themselves have been accused of misconduct and human rights abuses, highlighting the need for better training and accountability mechanisms.

Impact and Future Prospects:

Despite its imperfections, UN peacekeeping has made significant contributions to global peace and security. It has successfully facilitated the end of conflicts, promoted reconciliation, and protected civilians. The UN's involvement in humanitarian aid and disaster relief has also been instrumental in providing assistance to vulnerable populations during times of crisis.

Looking ahead, the UN is committed to enhancing the effectiveness of peacekeeping through ongoing reforms and improvements. Efforts to promote education, literacy, and sustainable development goals are also being integrated into peacekeeping operations, recognizing the interconnected nature of peace, development, and security.

Conclusion:

The history and evolution of UN peacekeeping underscore the vital role that the UN plays in maintaining peace and security worldwide. While challenges and criticisms exist, the successes of UN peacekeeping missions cannot be overlooked. As the world continues to grapple with complex conflicts and global challenges, the UN's role in promoting international cooperation, diplomacy, and sustainable development remains indispensable.

Peacekeeping in Action: Case Studies of Successful Missions

In the realm of international peacekeeping, the United Nations has played a vital role in resolving conflicts and restoring stability in war-torn regions. This subchapter, titled "Peacekeeping in Action: Case Studies of Successful Missions," delves into some notable examples of the United Nations' peacekeeping efforts and their impact on global peace and security.

One of the most significant success stories in United Nations peacekeeping is the mission in Sierra Leone. In the 1990s, the country was ravaged by a brutal civil war that left thousands dead and displaced millions. The United Nations Peacekeeping Force deployed to Sierra Leone, known as UNAMSIL, successfully disarmed rebel groups, stabilized the country, and facilitated the peaceful transition to democracy. This case study showcases the effectiveness of the United Nations in restoring peace in a conflict-ridden nation.

Another compelling example is the United Nations' peacekeeping mission in East Timor. Following the country's independence referendum in 1999, violent clashes erupted, leading to mass killings and widespread destruction. The United Nations Transitional Administration in East Timor (UNTAET) was established to restore peace and stability. Through its efforts, the mission facilitated the establishment of democratic institutions, built local capacity, and ensured the safe return of refugees. This success story demonstrates the United Nations' commitment to supporting nations in their transition to peace and self-governance.

Furthermore, the United Nations' peacekeeping mission in Liberia serves as an inspiration. The mission, known as UNMIL, was established in 2003 to help the country recover from a devastating civil war. Through its comprehensive approach, UNMIL supported disarmament, demobilization, and reintegration initiatives, promoted the rule of law, and facilitated free and fair elections. As a result, Liberia has made significant strides towards stability, and its people have been able to rebuild their lives.

These case studies highlight the United Nations' successes in peacekeeping and its crucial role in promoting global peace and security. By intervening in conflict zones, the organization has not only prevented further violence but also laid the foundation for sustainable development and prosperity. Through its missions, the United Nations has demonstrated its commitment to upholding human rights, promoting democracy, and fostering reconciliation.

As diplomats, scholars, educators, journalists, politicians, and members of the public, it is essential to recognize and celebrate the achievements of the United Nations in peacekeeping. By doing so, we can gain a deeper understanding of the organization's impact and inspire further support for its efforts. These case studies are a testament to the United Nations' tireless work and its ability to make a tangible difference in the lives of people affected by conflict.

Challenges and Limitations of UN Peacekeeping Operations

Peacekeeping operations are an integral part of the United Nations' efforts to maintain international peace and security. However, they are not without their challenges and limitations. In this subchapter, we will explore some of the key challenges faced by UN peacekeeping operations and the limitations that can hinder their effectiveness.

One of the major challenges faced by UN peacekeeping operations is the lack of adequate resources. Peacekeepers often operate in hostile environments with limited access to necessary equipment, personnel, and funding. This can hamper their ability to effectively carry out their mandate and protect civilians.

Another challenge is the complexity of conflicts. Peacekeepers often find themselves in situations where the lines between warring parties are blurred, making it difficult to distinguish between combatants and civilians. This can lead to challenges in enforcing peace agreements and protecting innocent lives.

Additionally, UN peacekeeping operations often face resistance from parties involved in the conflict. This can manifest in the form of non-compliance with peace agreements, attacks on peacekeepers, or the denial of access to certain areas. Such resistance can undermine the effectiveness of peacekeeping operations and hinder their ability to bring about lasting peace.

Another limitation of UN peacekeeping operations is the lack of a clear exit strategy. Peacekeeping missions are often deployed for extended periods, with no clear timeline for withdrawal. This can lead to a sense of dependency on international forces and can hinder the development of local capacities for conflict resolution and peacebuilding.

Furthermore, there is a need to improve the gender balance within peacekeeping operations. Despite efforts to promote gender equality and women's empowerment, women continue to be underrepresented in peacekeeping missions. This limits the ability of peacekeepers to fully understand and address the specific needs and concerns of women in conflict-affected areas.

Lastly, the effectiveness of UN peacekeeping operations is often hindered by political constraints and lack of consensus among member states. The Security Council, which authorizes and oversees peacekeeping missions, is often divided along political lines, making it difficult to take decisive action when needed.

In conclusion, while UN peacekeeping operations have made significant contributions to global peace and security, they face numerous challenges and limitations. Addressing these challenges and finding ways to overcome them is essential to ensure the effectiveness and sustainability of future peacekeeping efforts. The international community must come together to provide the necessary resources, support, and political will to enable UN peacekeeping operations to fulfill their mandate and bring about lasting peace in conflict-affected regions.

Evaluating the Effectiveness of UN Peacekeeping Missions
Introduction:
Peacekeeping missions are a crucial tool employed by the United Nations (UN) to maintain international peace and security. This subchapter aims to evaluate the effectiveness of UN peacekeeping missions and shed light on both their successes and imperfections.

By analyzing their impact, it becomes apparent how these missions contribute to the broader goals of the UN in promoting peace and stability worldwide.

Evaluation of Effectiveness:

UN peacekeeping missions have played a significant role in resolving conflicts and preventing the outbreak of new ones. By deploying troops, observers, and police personnel, the UN has successfully mediated ceasefires, promoted dialogue, and facilitated the transfer of power in numerous conflict zones. These missions have not only reduced violence and protected civilians but have also laid the groundwork for long-term peace and reconciliation.

However, it is important to acknowledge the imperfections and challenges faced by these missions. The UN's dependence on member states for resources, including troops and funding, often limits their effectiveness. Additionally, the impartiality and neutrality of peacekeepers have been questioned in some instances, leading to a loss of credibility. The subchapter will explore these limitations and propose recommendations for improvement.

Significance for Various Audiences:

Diplomats, scholars, educators, journalists, politicians, and the public can benefit from understanding the effectiveness of UN peacekeeping missions. Diplomats and politicians can utilize this knowledge to enhance their decision-making processes regarding peacekeeping interventions. Scholars and educators can incorporate these insights into their research and teaching, fostering a better understanding of the complexities involved. Journalists can provide accurate and comprehensive reporting on UN peacekeeping missions, contributing to informed public opinion.

Furthermore, this evaluation is relevant to the niches of the United Nations' successes, as it demonstrates the organization's commitment to maintaining international peace and security. It also aligns with the UN's efforts in promoting gender equality, addressing global health challenges, combating climate change, reducing poverty, promoting human rights, providing humanitarian aid, promoting education, and fostering international cooperation and diplomacy.

Conclusion:

Evaluating the effectiveness of UN peacekeeping missions is crucial for understanding the successes and limitations of this key tool in maintaining global peace and security. By comprehending their impact, diplomats, scholars, educators, journalists, politicians, and the public can contribute to strengthening these missions and ultimately achieving the broader goals of the United Nations.

The Role of Member States in Supporting Peacekeeping Efforts

One of the key pillars of the United Nations' work is peacekeeping, and the success of these missions heavily relies on the support and cooperation of member states. Throughout its history, the UN has played a crucial role in resolving conflicts and maintaining peace in various regions around the world. However, the effectiveness of peacekeeping missions largely depends on the commitment and contributions of member states.

Member states play a vital role in supporting peacekeeping efforts by providing financial resources, troops, and logistical support. Financial contributions are essential for the UN to maintain and sustain peacekeeping operations. Diplomats, politicians, and scholars understand that peacekeeping missions can be costly, both in terms of human lives and financial resources. Therefore, member states' financial commitment is crucial to ensure the smooth functioning of these operations.

Moreover, member states' provision of troops and personnel is crucial for the success of peacekeeping missions. Member states can contribute military personnel, police officers, and civilian experts to these missions. Their presence on the ground helps maintain stability, protect civilians, and support the political process in conflict-affected areas.

In addition to troops and financial support, member states also provide logistical support to peacekeeping operations. This includes transportation, communication, and medical assistance, among other essential services. Diplomats, journalists, and educators recognize that without proper logistical support, peacekeeping missions would struggle to effectively carry out their mandates.

Furthermore, member states also have a role to play in shaping the policies and strategies of peacekeeping missions. Through their participation in the General Assembly, Security Council, and other relevant bodies, member states can contribute to the decision-making process and ensure that peacekeeping efforts align with the UN's goals and principles.

In conclusion, member states are integral to the success of United Nations peacekeeping efforts. Their financial contributions, provision of troops, logistical support, and active participation in decision-making processes are essential for maintaining peace and stability in conflict-affected regions. Diplomats, scholars, educators, journalists, politicians, and the public play a crucial role in advocating for the necessary support and resources to strengthen the UN's peacekeeping capabilities. By recognizing and appreciating the role of member states, we can continue to celebrate the successes of the United Nations while acknowledging its imperfections and working towards a more peaceful and just world.

Chapter 3: United Nations' Efforts in Promoting Gender Equality and Women's Empowerment

Gender Equality: A Fundamental Principle of the United Nations

Gender equality is one of the fundamental principles that underpin the work of the United Nations (UN). The organization has been committed to promoting gender equality and women's empowerment since its inception. In fact, the UN Charter, signed in 1945, explicitly states the principle of gender equality as a core value.

The UN recognizes that achieving gender equality is not only a human rights issue but also a necessary condition for sustainable development, peace, and security. Gender equality is essential for building inclusive societies, eradicating poverty, and ensuring the well-being of all individuals, regardless of their gender.

Over the years, the UN has implemented various initiatives to promote gender equality and women's empowerment. One of the landmark achievements is the adoption of the Convention on the Elimination of All Forms of Discrimination Against Women (CEDAW) in 1979. This international treaty sets out the obligations of states to eliminate discrimination against women in all aspects of life, including politics, education, employment, and health.

The UN has also established specialized agencies, such as UN Women, to focus on gender equality and women's rights. These agencies work towards advancing gender equality through policy advocacy, capacity building, and resource mobilization. They also support countries in implementing gender-responsive policies and programs.

In addition, the UN has launched global campaigns, such as the HeForShe campaign, to engage men and boys as allies in the fight for gender equality. The organization recognizes that gender equality is a shared responsibility that requires the active involvement of all members of society.

The UN's commitment to gender equality is evident in its Sustainable Development Goals (SDGs). Goal 5 specifically aims to achieve gender equality and empower all women and girls. This goal includes targets such as ending all forms of discrimination against women, eliminating violence against women, ensuring women's full participation in decision-making, and providing universal access to sexual and reproductive health.

While significant progress has been made, challenges remain in achieving gender equality worldwide. The UN continues to work towards addressing these challenges through policy advocacy, capacity building, and partnerships with governments, civil society organizations, and the private sector.

In conclusion, gender equality is a fundamental principle of the United Nations. The organization recognizes that achieving gender equality is not only a matter of human rights but also a necessary condition for sustainable development, peace, and security. Through its various initiatives and campaigns, the UN is committed to promoting gender equality and women's empowerment worldwide. However, more efforts are needed to overcome the existing challenges and ensure that gender equality becomes a reality for all.

The United Nations' Commitment to Women's Rights

In the quest for gender equality and women's empowerment, the United Nations has been at the forefront, tirelessly working towards creating a more inclusive and equitable world. Recognizing that women's rights are human rights, the UN has made significant strides in promoting gender equality and empowering women worldwide.

One of the key achievements of the United Nations in this regard has been the adoption of the Convention on the Elimination of All Forms of Discrimination Against Women (CEDAW) in 1979. This landmark treaty has provided a comprehensive framework for advancing women's rights, addressing issues such as violence against women, discrimination in employment, and access to education and healthcare. Today, an impressive 189 countries have ratified CEDAW, demonstrating their commitment to promoting gender equality.

The UN has also established several entities and initiatives dedicated to advancing women's rights. The UN Women, created in 2010, has played a crucial role in advocating for gender equality and promoting women's empowerment. Through its programs and campaigns, UN Women works towards eliminating gender-based violence, enhancing women's economic empowerment, and ensuring women's participation in decision-making processes at all levels.

Furthermore, the United Nations has consistently emphasized the importance of women's representation and participation in peace and security processes. The landmark Security Council Resolution 1325, adopted in 2000, recognizes the critical role women play in conflict prevention, resolution, and peacebuilding. By promoting women's inclusion in peacekeeping missions and peace negotiations, the UN is striving to create more sustainable and inclusive peace.

The United Nations has also been instrumental in promoting women's health and addressing global health challenges. Through initiatives like the Global Strategy for Women's, Children's, and Adolescents' Health, the UN focuses on improving access to reproductive healthcare, reducing maternal mortality, and combating HIV/AIDS. Additionally, the UN works towards eliminating harmful practices such as female genital mutilation and child marriage, which pose significant threats to women's rights and well-being.

In conclusion, the United Nations has demonstrated a strong commitment to women's rights and gender equality. Through international treaties, dedicated entities, and initiatives, the UN has made significant progress in empowering women and promoting their rights. However, challenges still remain, and the UN continues to work towards creating a more inclusive and equitable world for women.

Advancing Women's Political Participation and Leadership

In recent years, there has been a growing recognition of the importance of gender equality and women's empowerment in all aspects of global development. One area where progress has been made is in advancing women's political participation and leadership. The United Nations (UN) has played a vital role in promoting and supporting initiatives aimed at empowering women in politics and leadership positions around the world.

The UN has been a strong advocate for the inclusion of women in decision-making processes at all levels of government. It has called for the removal of legal and social barriers that prevent women from participating fully in political and public life. Through its various agencies and programs, the UN has provided technical assistance, capacity building, and funding to support women's political participation.

One of the notable successes of the UN in this area is the adoption of the Convention on the Elimination of All Forms of Discrimination against Women (CEDAW). This international treaty has been instrumental in promoting women's rights and has led to the establishment of national mechanisms to promote gender equality and women's empowerment.

The UN has also supported women's political leadership through initiatives such as the Women's Leadership and Political Participation initiative. This program aims to increase the number of women in leadership positions by providing training and mentorship opportunities for women interested in politics.

Furthermore, the UN has partnered with governments, civil society organizations, and other stakeholders to promote gender-responsive governance. This involves working towards gender balance in decision-making processes, ensuring that women's perspectives and needs are taken into account in policy development and implementation.

Despite these successes, challenges remain in advancing women's political participation and leadership. Deep-rooted gender norms, stereotypes, and discrimination continue to hinder women's progress in this area. The UN continues to work towards addressing these challenges through awareness-raising campaigns, advocacy efforts, and capacity-building programs.

In conclusion, the UN has made significant strides in advancing women's political participation and leadership. Through its various initiatives, it has worked towards breaking down barriers and creating opportunities for women to participate fully in political and public life. However, there is still much work to be done to achieve gender equality in this realm. With continued collaboration and commitment from governments, civil society, and the public, we can build a more inclusive and equitable world where women's voices are heard and their leadership is valued.

Empowering Women Economically: Initiatives and Success Stories
Introduction:
In recent years, the United Nations has taken significant steps to promote gender equality and women's empowerment globally. Recognizing the crucial role women play in economic development, the organization has implemented various initiatives to support and enhance women's economic participation. This subchapter delves into the initiatives and success stories that highlight the progress made in empowering women economically.

Initiatives:
The United Nations has launched several initiatives to promote economic empowerment for women. One such initiative is the Women's Empowerment Principles (WEPs), a joint effort by the UN Global Compact and UN Women. WEPs provide guidelines for businesses to promote gender equality in the workplace, supply chain, and community. Through WEPs, companies can create inclusive workplaces that offer equal opportunities for women to thrive.

Another initiative, the UN Women's Empowerment Principles for Access to Markets, focuses on improving women's economic opportunities through access to markets and trade. By enhancing women's entrepreneurship, access to finance, and participation in decision-making processes, this initiative aims to break down barriers hindering women's economic empowerment.

Success Stories:

The United Nations' initiatives have yielded remarkable success stories in empowering women economically. One such story is the case of Rwanda, where the UN supported the government in implementing gender-responsive budgeting. This initiative facilitated the allocation of resources towards programs that directly impacted women's economic opportunities, resulting in increased access to education, healthcare, and entrepreneurship for Rwandan women.

In India, the UN's partnership with Self Employed Women's Association (SEWA) has empowered millions of women in the informal sector. Through training, capacity building, and access to finance, SEWA has enabled women to establish and scale their businesses, improving their livelihoods and contributing to the local economy.

In Colombia, the UN has worked closely with the government to promote women's economic empowerment in conflict-affected areas. By providing skills training, access to credit, and support for income-generating projects, women in these regions have been able to rebuild their lives and contribute to the local economy, promoting peace and stability.

Conclusion:

The United Nations has played a pivotal role in advancing women's economic empowerment globally. Through initiatives like the Women's Empowerment Principles and partnerships with local organizations, the UN has succeeded in breaking down barriers and creating opportunities for women to thrive economically. The success stories emerging from countries like Rwanda, India, and Colombia demonstrate the tangible impact of these initiatives on women's lives and the broader society. As we celebrate the successes achieved thus far, it is crucial to continue supporting and strengthening these initiatives, ensuring that every woman has the opportunity to participate fully in the global economy. By empowering women economically, we not only enhance their lives but also contribute to sustainable development and a more equal and just world for all.

Combating Violence against Women: UN Efforts and Achievements

Violence against women is a global issue that requires concerted efforts from governments, institutions, and civil society to address and eradicate. The United Nations has been at the forefront of this fight, championing the cause and implementing various initiatives to combat violence against women. This subchapter explores the UN's efforts and achievements in this crucial area.

The UN has adopted a comprehensive approach to addressing violence against women, recognizing that it is not just a violation of human rights but also a barrier to development and peace. Through its various entities and programs, the UN has worked towards raising awareness, advocating for policy changes, and providing support to survivors.

One of the key achievements of the UN in combating violence against women is the adoption of the landmark Convention on the Elimination of All Forms of Discrimination against Women (CEDAW). This international treaty sets out the obligations of states parties to prevent, investigate, and punish violence against women. The CEDAW has been ratified by almost all UN member states, making it a powerful tool in the fight against gender-based violence.

The UN has also established the UN Women entity, which focuses on promoting gender equality and women's empowerment. UN Women works closely with governments, NGOs, and grassroots organizations to implement programs that address violence against women. Through its initiatives, UN Women has supported the establishment of shelters, helplines, and legal aid services for survivors, as well as campaigns to change social norms and attitudes towards violence against women.

Moreover, the UN has launched the "UNiTE to End Violence against Women" campaign, which aims to raise public awareness and mobilize political will to end violence against women and girls. This campaign urges governments to enact and enforce laws that protect women and provides funding and technical assistance to countries to implement comprehensive strategies to combat violence.

Additionally, the UN has played a crucial role in promoting the inclusion of gender-based violence in the international development agenda. The Sustainable Development Goals (SDGs), adopted by all UN member states in 2015, include a specific target to end all forms of violence against women and girls. The UN has been working with governments and stakeholders to monitor progress towards this target and ensure that violence against women is prioritized in national policies and programs.

In conclusion, the UN has made significant efforts and achieved notable milestones in combating violence against women. Through its various entities, campaigns, and initiatives, the UN has raised awareness, advocated for policy changes, and provided support to survivors. However, the fight is far from over, and continued collaboration and commitment from all stakeholders are essential to achieve a world free from violence against women.

Chapter 4: United Nations' Role in Addressing Global Health Challenges

The United Nations' Global Health Mandate

In today's interconnected world, the need for global cooperation to address health challenges has never been more evident. The United Nations (UN) has recognized this need and has taken on a significant role in promoting global health initiatives. This subchapter will explore the UN's global health mandate and its efforts to ensure the well-being of people worldwide.

The UN's global health mandate is rooted in its commitment to promote and protect the right to health for all individuals. It recognizes that health is a fundamental human right and an essential component of sustainable development. Through various agencies and programs, the UN works towards achieving universal health coverage, addressing communicable and non-communicable diseases, and improving maternal and child health.

One of the key initiatives under the UN's global health mandate is the World Health Organization (WHO). The WHO plays a central role in coordinating international efforts to prevent and respond to health emergencies, such as pandemics and outbreaks. It provides technical assistance to member states, conducts research, and sets global health standards and guidelines.

Additionally, the UN's global health mandate extends beyond the WHO. It encompasses other UN agencies, such as UNICEF, UNAIDS, and the United Nations Population Fund (UNFPA), which work together to address specific health issues. These agencies focus on areas such as HIV/AIDS prevention, immunization, access to clean water and sanitation, and sexual and reproductive health.

The UN's commitment to global health is not limited to addressing diseases and health emergencies. It also recognizes the importance of social determinants of health, such as poverty, education, and gender equality. Through the Sustainable Development Goals (SDGs), the UN aims to improve health outcomes by addressing these underlying factors. For example, SDG 3 focuses on ensuring healthy lives and promoting well-being for all at all ages.

In conclusion, the UN's global health mandate is a critical aspect of its broader mission to promote peace, development, and human rights. By recognizing health as a fundamental human right, the UN works towards achieving universal health coverage, addressing diseases, and improving overall well-being. Through its various agencies, programs, and initiatives, the UN strives to create a healthier and more equitable world for all.

The World Health Organization: A Vital UN Agency

The World Health Organization (WHO) is a crucial agency within the United Nations system, playing a vital role in addressing global health challenges. With a mission to promote the highest possible level of health for all people, the WHO has made significant contributions to improving public health worldwide.

One of the key achievements of the WHO is its role in eradicating and controlling diseases. The organization has successfully led efforts to eliminate smallpox, a devastating disease that plagued humanity for centuries. Through its immunization programs, the WHO has also made significant progress in reducing the prevalence of polio, measles, and other vaccine-preventable diseases, saving millions of lives in the process.

In addition to disease eradication, the WHO has been at the forefront of responding to global health emergencies. From the Ebola outbreak in West Africa to the Zika virus epidemic, the organization has provided leadership, coordination, and technical expertise to support affected countries in controlling the spread of diseases and minimizing their impact.

Furthermore, the WHO has played a crucial role in promoting health equity and addressing the social determinants of health. By advocating for universal healthcare coverage and access to essential medicines, the organization has helped to reduce health disparities and improve health outcomes for vulnerable populations.

The WHO also actively contributes to research and development in the field of global health. Through its partnerships with academic institutions, governments, and other stakeholders, the organization promotes the sharing of knowledge and best practices, leading to innovative approaches in disease prevention, treatment, and healthcare delivery.

Moreover, the WHO plays a critical role in shaping international health policies and standards. By providing evidence-based guidance and recommendations, the organization influences decision-making processes at the national and global levels, ensuring that health considerations are integrated into various sectors, such as trade, agriculture, and environment.

In conclusion, the World Health Organization is an indispensable UN agency that has made significant contributions to global health. From disease eradication to emergency response, the WHO has demonstrated its effectiveness in addressing health challenges. Through its leadership, technical expertise, and advocacy, the organization continues to play a vital role in improving the health and well-being of people worldwide. As we celebrate the successes of the United Nations, we must recognize the critical role of the WHO in achieving the goal of health for all.

United Nations' Initiatives in Disease Prevention and Control
Introduction:
Disease prevention and control has always been a top priority for the United Nations (UN) as it directly affects the well-being and development of nations. Over the years, the UN has spearheaded various initiatives to combat deadly diseases and promote public health

worldwide. This subchapter aims to shed light on the UN's efforts in disease prevention and control and highlight some of its successful initiatives.

Body:

1. Global Health Initiatives:

The UN has played a pivotal role in coordinating global health efforts through organizations such as the World Health Organization (WHO). These initiatives include immunization campaigns, disease surveillance systems, and the development of vaccines for diseases like polio, measles, and Ebola. The UN's strong focus on preventive measures has significantly reduced the burden of diseases, saving countless lives.

2. Pandemic Preparedness:

The UN has been at the forefront of preparing for and responding to pandemics. The establishment of the Global Outbreak Alert and Response Network (GOARN) and the UN System Influenza Coordinator (UNSIC) has enhanced global coordination and response mechanisms. These initiatives proved crucial during the H1N1 influenza pandemic and the recent COVID-19 outbreak.

3. Access to Essential Medicines:

Recognizing the importance of affordable and accessible medicines, the UN has been actively promoting the use of generic drugs and supporting countries in strengthening their pharmaceutical supply chains. Through initiatives like the Medicines Patent Pool and the Global Fund to Fight AIDS, Tuberculosis, and Malaria, the UN has made significant progress in improving access to essential medicines in developing countries.

4. Behavioral Change and Health Promotion:

The UN has been instrumental in promoting behavioral change and health education to prevent the spread of diseases. Initiatives like the Global Handwashing Day and the Tobacco-Free Initiative have raised awareness about the importance of hygiene and the harmful effects of tobacco. These efforts have resulted in positive changes in people's attitudes and behaviors towards disease prevention.

Conclusion:

The United Nations' initiatives in disease prevention and control reflect its commitment to improving global health outcomes. From promoting immunization to preparing for pandemics and ensuring access to essential medicines, the UN has made remarkable progress in safeguarding public health. However, challenges remain, and the UN continues to work towards new strategies and partnerships to address emerging health threats. By highlighting these initiatives, this subchapter aims to inspire and encourage further collaboration in disease prevention and control efforts, ultimately contributing to a healthier and safer world for all.

Tackling Global Health Inequalities: Access to Healthcare for All

In the quest for a more equitable and inclusive world, one of the most pressing challenges we face is ensuring access to healthcare for all. The United Nations has been at the forefront of efforts to tackle global health inequalities, recognizing that every individual, regardless of their background or circumstances, deserves the right to quality healthcare.

Access to healthcare is not just a matter of social justice; it is a fundamental human right. Unfortunately, millions of people around the world still lack access to basic healthcare services, leading to unnecessary suffering and preventable deaths. This is particularly evident in developing countries where poverty, inadequate infrastructure, and limited resources pose significant barriers to healthcare access.

The United Nations has taken on the responsibility of addressing these disparities head-on. Through its various agencies, such as the World Health Organization (WHO), the UN has implemented a range of initiatives aimed at improving healthcare access for all. These initiatives include advocating for universal health coverage, strengthening healthcare systems in developing countries, and addressing the social determinants of health.

One of the UN's notable achievements in this area is the development of the Sustainable Development Goals (SDGs). Goal 3 specifically focuses on ensuring healthy lives and promoting well-being for all at all ages. Under this goal, the UN aims to achieve universal health coverage, including access to essential healthcare services, vaccines, and medicines by 2030.

To achieve this ambitious goal, the UN has been working closely with governments, civil society organizations, and other stakeholders to mobilize resources, build capacity, and foster international cooperation. Through partnerships and collaborations, the UN has helped to strengthen healthcare systems, improve access to medicines, and promote health education and prevention programs.

However, despite these efforts, significant challenges remain. Health inequalities persist, particularly for marginalized populations, women, children, and people living in remote or conflict-affected areas. To address these challenges, the UN continues to advocate for increased investment in healthcare infrastructure, improved training and retention of healthcare professionals, and the removal of barriers to access, such as discrimination and stigma.

In conclusion, the United Nations has played a crucial role in addressing global health inequalities and promoting access to healthcare for all. Through its commitment to the SDGs and its efforts to strengthen healthcare systems, the UN has made significant progress in improving health outcomes worldwide. However, more work is needed to ensure that no one is left behind, and that access to quality healthcare becomes a reality for all. By continuing to prioritize healthcare as a fundamental right, we can build a healthier, more equitable world for future generations.

The United Nations' Response to Global Health Emergencies

In the face of global health emergencies, the United Nations (UN) has played a vital role in coordinating international efforts and providing crucial support to affected countries. This subchapter explores the UN's response to such emergencies and highlights its successes and imperfections in addressing these challenges.

The UN's response to global health emergencies is guided by its commitment to promoting health as a fundamental human right. The World Health Organization (WHO), a specialized agency of the UN, takes the lead in coordinating the response to outbreaks and pandemics. Through its Global Outbreak Alert and Response Network, the WHO provides rapid response teams, technical expertise, and resources to affected countries.

One of the UN's notable successes in responding to global health emergencies is its role in tackling the Ebola outbreak in West Africa in 2014. The UN, in collaboration with international partners, mobilized resources and expertise to control the spread of the virus, treat the affected, and support the recovery efforts. This coordinated response helped to contain the outbreak and save lives.

However, the UN also faces challenges and imperfections in responding to global health emergencies. The COVID-19 pandemic, for instance, exposed gaps in global preparedness and response mechanisms. The UN has acknowledged the need for stronger coordination, timely information sharing, and increased investment in health systems to effectively respond to future emergencies.

To address these challenges, the UN has initiated various measures. It has called for increased funding for global health emergencies, strengthened partnerships with governments, civil society organizations, and the private sector, and advocated for equitable access to vaccines, diagnostics, and treatments. The UN has also emphasized the importance of investing in resilient health systems, ensuring universal health coverage, and prioritizing prevention and preparedness.

Moving forward, the UN continues to play a crucial role in strengthening global health security. It is actively involved in promoting research and development, advancing knowledge sharing, and supporting countries in building their capacity to prevent, detect, and respond to health emergencies. The UN's response to global health emergencies remains an ongoing effort, reflecting its commitment to protecting the health and well-being of people worldwide.

In conclusion, the UN's response to global health emergencies is a testament to its successes and imperfections. While it has achieved significant milestones in addressing outbreaks and pandemics, challenges persist. By learning from past experiences, strengthening collaboration, and prioritizing global health security, the UN continues to work towards a safer, healthier, and more resilient world.

Chapter 5: United Nations' Initiatives in Combating Climate Change and Environmental Sustainability

Climate Change: A Global Crisis Requiring Collective Action

Climate change is undeniably one of the most pressing challenges of our time. Its impacts are felt across the globe, from rising sea levels and extreme weather events to widespread biodiversity loss and food insecurity. Recognizing the urgency of this crisis, the international community has come together under the auspices of the United Nations to address climate change and promote environmental sustainability.

The United Nations, through various initiatives and agreements, has played a pivotal role in mobilizing global action to combat climate change. The Paris Agreement, signed in 2015, stands as a landmark achievement in this regard. It brought together nearly 200 countries, setting ambitious targets to limit global temperature rise and enhance adaptive capacity. The agreement also established a framework for financial and technological support to developing countries, recognizing the principle of common but differentiated responsibilities.

The United Nations Framework Convention on Climate Change (UNFCCC) serves as the central platform for international cooperation on climate change. Through its annual Conference of the Parties (COP), countries negotiate and adopt measures to reduce greenhouse gas emissions, promote sustainable development, and adapt to the impacts of climate change. These negotiations bring together not only diplomats and politicians but also scientists, scholars, educators, and journalists, fostering a comprehensive and inclusive dialogue on climate action.

Moreover, the United Nations has launched several initiatives to promote environmental sustainability and combat climate change. The Sustainable Development Goals (SDGs), adopted in 2015, include a specific goal on climate action (SDG 13) and integrate climate considerations across all goals. The United Nations Environment Programme (UNEP) works to coordinate global efforts in environmental protection and climate change mitigation, providing technical expertise and support to member states.

Addressing climate change requires collective action at all levels, from individual choices to national policies and international cooperation. The United Nations, as a global organization, plays a crucial role in facilitating this collective action. By promoting knowledge exchange, capacity building, and resource mobilization, the United Nations empowers governments, civil society, and the public to take effective measures to mitigate and adapt to climate change.

In conclusion, climate change represents a global crisis that demands collective action. The United Nations, through its various initiatives and agreements, has spearheaded global efforts to combat climate change and promote environmental sustainability. By bringing together diplomats, scholars, educators, journalists, politicians, and the public, the United Nations fosters dialogue and collaboration to address this urgent challenge. However, the fight against climate change is an ongoing process, and continued global cooperation is essential to ensure a sustainable and resilient future for all.

The United Nations Framework Convention on Climate Change

The United Nations Framework Convention on Climate Change (UNFCCC) is a landmark agreement that aims to address the urgent issue of climate change on a global scale. As part of the book "United Nations: Celebrating Successes and Imperfections", this subchapter delves into the UNFCCC's role in promoting environmental sustainability and combating climate change.

DIPLOMATS, SCHOLARS, EDUCATORS, JOURNALISTS, POLITICIANS, THE PUBLIC

The United Nations Framework Convention on Climate Change (UNFCCC) is a significant achievement in the United Nations' efforts to combat climate change and promote environmental sustainability. Established in 1992, the UNFCCC seeks to stabilize greenhouse gas concentrations in the atmosphere at a level that will prevent dangerous human-induced interference with the climate system.

One of the key successes of the UNFCCC is the adoption of the Kyoto Protocol in 1997, which set binding emission reduction targets for developed countries. This marked an important step towards addressing the root causes of climate change and promoting international cooperation in reducing greenhouse gas emissions.

Since then, the UNFCCC has played a crucial role in facilitating global climate negotiations, including the historic Paris Agreement in 2015. The Paris Agreement aims to limit global warming to well below 2 degrees Celsius above pre-industrial levels and to pursue efforts to limit the temperature increase to 1.5 degrees Celsius. It also emphasizes the need for financial support to developing countries to enhance their ability to mitigate and adapt to climate change.

The UNFCCC has also been instrumental in promoting climate change adaptation and resilience-building efforts worldwide. It provides a platform for countries to share their experiences, best practices, and challenges in adapting to the impacts of climate change, such as rising sea levels, extreme weather events, and food insecurity.

Furthermore, the UNFCCC has been actively engaging with various stakeholders, including civil society organizations, the private sector, and the scientific community, to mobilize collective action in addressing climate change. This inclusive approach recognizes that tackling climate change requires the collaboration and commitment of all sectors of society.

While the UNFCCC has made significant strides in addressing climate change, it also acknowledges the imperfections and challenges that lie ahead. The urgency to accelerate climate action, enhance climate finance, and strengthen international cooperation remains paramount in achieving the goals set out in the Paris Agreement.

In conclusion, the United Nations Framework Convention on Climate Change has played a pivotal role in promoting global efforts to combat climate change and ensure environmental sustainability. Its successes, such as the adoption of the Kyoto Protocol and the Paris Agreement, demonstrate the UN's commitment to addressing one of the most pressing challenges of our time. However, continued collaboration and collective action are needed to overcome the imperfections and achieve a sustainable and resilient future for all.

The Paris Agreement: A Landmark Achievement

The Paris Agreement stands as a testament to the power of international cooperation and diplomacy in addressing one of the most pressing global challenges of our time: climate change. Signed in 2015, this historic accord represents a significant milestone in the United Nations' initiatives in combating climate change and promoting environmental sustainability.

The Paris Agreement aims to limit global warming to well below 2 degrees Celsius above pre-industrial levels and to pursue efforts to limit the temperature increase to 1.5 degrees Celsius. It recognizes the urgent need to reduce greenhouse gas emissions and outlines a framework for countries to set their own targets and implement strategies to achieve them. By establishing a transparent system for monitoring progress and reporting on emissions, the agreement ensures accountability and encourages countries to continuously raise their ambitions.

This landmark achievement has far-reaching implications for all stakeholders. For diplomats, it demonstrates the power of multilateralism and the effectiveness of collective action in addressing global challenges. It reaffirms the United Nations' role in promoting international cooperation and diplomacy as key tools for achieving common goals.

Scholars and educators can draw valuable lessons from the Paris Agreement, highlighting the importance of scientific research and evidence-based decision-making in shaping effective environmental policies. The agreement also serves as an educational tool, raising awareness about the impacts of climate change and the urgent need for action among students and the wider public.

Journalists play a crucial role in disseminating information about the Paris Agreement and its implementation progress. By reporting on the achievements, challenges, and lessons learned, they can foster a greater understanding and engagement with climate change issues among the public.

Politicians have a responsibility to translate the goals of the Paris Agreement into concrete actions at the national level. By implementing policies that promote renewable energy, energy efficiency, and sustainable development, they can contribute to the global effort to combat climate change.

For the public, the Paris Agreement signifies hope for a sustainable future. It demonstrates that governments are committed to taking bold action to protect the planet and secure a better future for generations to come. By supporting and holding their governments accountable for the agreement's implementation, the public can actively contribute to achieving its objectives.

In conclusion, the Paris Agreement is a landmark achievement in the United Nations' initiatives to combat climate change and promote environmental sustainability. It serves as a powerful example of the organization's ability to bring nations together to address shared challenges. By acknowledging the significance of this achievement, we can celebrate the successes of the United Nations and work towards a more sustainable and just world for all.

Promoting Renewable Energy and Sustainable Development

Renewable energy and sustainable development have become crucial topics in today's world, as we face the challenges of climate change and environmental degradation. The United Nations has been at the forefront of promoting renewable energy and sustainable development, recognizing the importance of these initiatives in creating a better future for all.

One of the key initiatives undertaken by the United Nations is the promotion of renewable energy sources such as solar, wind, hydro, and geothermal power. Through various programs and partnerships, the UN has been working towards increasing the use of renewable energy globally. This includes providing technical assistance to countries in developing renewable energy projects, promoting investment in clean energy technologies, and facilitating knowledge sharing among member states.

In addition to promoting renewable energy, the United Nations is also actively involved in advancing sustainable development goals (SDGs). These goals aim to address various aspects of sustainable development, including poverty eradication, access to clean water and sanitation, sustainable cities and communities, and responsible consumption and production. The UN provides support to countries in implementing these goals through capacity-building programs, policy advice, and financial assistance.

Furthermore, the United Nations plays a crucial role in facilitating international cooperation and diplomacy in the field of renewable energy and sustainable development. Through platforms such as the United Nations Framework Convention on Climate Change (UNFCCC) and the Sustainable Development Goals (SDGs), member states come together to discuss and negotiate strategies for achieving a sustainable future. The UN also organizes conferences, summits, and workshops to promote dialogue and collaboration among stakeholders from governments, civil society, academia, and the private sector.

The efforts of the United Nations in promoting renewable energy and sustainable development are not only vital for addressing the pressing environmental challenges but also for achieving social and economic progress. By transitioning to cleaner and more sustainable energy sources, countries can reduce greenhouse gas emissions, improve air quality, create job opportunities, and enhance energy security.

In conclusion, the United Nations has been actively promoting renewable energy and sustainable development as crucial elements for a better future. Through various programs, partnerships, and initiatives, the UN is working towards increasing the use of renewable energy, advancing the SDGs, and fostering international cooperation. It is imperative for diplomats, scholars, educators, journalists, politicians, and the public to recognize and support these efforts, as they are essential for creating a sustainable and prosperous world for generations to come.

Protecting Biodiversity: UN Efforts and Conservation Successes

Biodiversity is crucial for the health and resilience of our planet, providing numerous benefits such as ecosystem stability, food security, and climate regulation. Recognizing the urgent need to protect and conserve biodiversity, the United Nations has played a significant role in spearheading global efforts in this area. This subchapter explores the UN's initiatives and conservation successes in protecting biodiversity.

The United Nations has been instrumental in creating awareness and advocating for the conservation of biodiversity. Through its various agencies, such as the United Nations Environment Programme (UNEP) and the Convention on Biological Diversity (CBD), the UN has been at the forefront of promoting sustainable practices and raising awareness about the importance of biodiversity.

One of the notable achievements of the UN in biodiversity conservation is the establishment of protected areas. The UN has supported the creation of national parks, marine reserves, and other protected areas worldwide, contributing to the preservation of unique ecosystems and endangered species. These protected areas serve as essential habitats for a wide range of flora and fauna, ensuring their survival for future generations.

Furthermore, the UN has facilitated international cooperation and collaboration in biodiversity conservation. It has encouraged countries to work together to develop strategies, share knowledge, and implement conservation measures. The UN's initiatives have fostered partnerships among governments, NGOs, and local communities, promoting a holistic approach to biodiversity protection.

The UN's efforts have also resulted in several conservation successes. For instance, the UN's collaboration with local communities in Costa Rica led to the successful restoration of degraded ecosystems and the recovery of endangered species. In Rwanda, the UN's support for community-based conservation initiatives helped protect mountain gorillas and their habitats.

Despite these successes, challenges remain in protecting biodiversity. Habitat loss, climate change, pollution, and illegal wildlife trade continue to pose significant threats. The UN continues to address these challenges by promoting sustainable development and integrating biodiversity conservation into national and international policies.

In conclusion, the United Nations has been a driving force in protecting and conserving biodiversity. Through its initiatives, the UN has raised awareness, fostered international cooperation, and achieved notable successes in biodiversity conservation. However, continued efforts and collaboration are essential to ensure the long-term preservation of our planet's rich biodiversity. By working together, we can secure a sustainable future for all species and ecosystems.

Chapter 6: United Nations' Contribution to International Development and Poverty Reduction

The United Nations' Commitment to Sustainable Development

Sustainable development has become a key focus for the United Nations, as it recognizes the urgent need to balance economic growth, social progress, and environmental protection. The organization has made significant strides in promoting sustainable development goals (SDGs) and has become a leading voice in addressing global challenges.

One of the United Nations' successes in sustainable development is its role in combatting climate change and promoting environmental sustainability. Through initiatives such as the Paris Agreement, the UN has been instrumental in bringing countries together to address the pressing issue of climate change. By setting ambitious targets and facilitating international cooperation, the organization has played a crucial role in reducing greenhouse gas emissions and promoting renewable energy.

Another area where the United Nations has made a significant impact is in promoting gender equality and women's empowerment. The organization has been at the forefront of advocating for women's rights and has made efforts to ensure equal opportunities for women in all spheres of life. Through initiatives such as the UN Women's Empowerment Principles and the HeForShe campaign, the UN has been working towards breaking down gender barriers and empowering women to participate fully in society.

The United Nations has also been actively involved in addressing global health challenges. With initiatives such as the World Health Organization (WHO), the UN has been at the forefront of coordinating international efforts to combat diseases and improve healthcare systems. The organization has played a critical role in responding to outbreaks such as Ebola and COVID-19, providing resources, expertise, and support to affected countries.

Furthermore, the United Nations has been a driving force in promoting international development and poverty reduction. Through programs such as the Millennium Development Goals and now the SDGs, the UN has been working towards eradicating poverty, improving education, and ensuring access to basic services for all. By mobilizing resources and advocating for sustainable development practices, the UN has helped lift millions of people out of poverty.

The United Nations' commitment to sustainable development is also evident in its promotion of human rights and global justice. The organization has been a strong advocate for human rights, working towards the protection and promotion of fundamental freedoms worldwide. Through mechanisms such as the Universal Declaration of Human Rights and the International Criminal Court, the UN has played a crucial role in holding states accountable for human rights violations and ensuring justice for victims.

The United Nations has also been actively involved in humanitarian aid and disaster relief efforts. Through agencies such as the United Nations High Commissioner for Refugees (UNHCR) and the United Nations Children's Fund (UNICEF), the UN has provided vital assistance to those affected by conflict, natural disasters, and other emergencies. By coordinating international efforts and mobilizing resources, the UN has saved countless lives and provided essential support to vulnerable populations.

Education and literacy are also areas where the United Nations has made a significant impact. Through initiatives such as UNESCO's Education for All and the Global Education First Initiative, the UN has been working towards ensuring quality education for all and promoting literacy worldwide. The organization recognizes that education is a fundamental right and a critical tool for sustainable development.

In conclusion, the United Nations' commitment to sustainable development is evident through its various initiatives and successes. From combatting climate change to promoting gender equality, the UN has been at the forefront of addressing global challenges. As diplomats, scholars, educators, journalists, politicians, and the public, we must recognize and support the UN's efforts to achieve a more sustainable and equitable world.

The Millennium Development Goals: Progress and Lessons Learned

In the pursuit of global progress and development, the United Nations set forth a set of ambitious goals known as the Millennium Development Goals (MDGs) in the year 2000. These goals were designed to address key challenges faced by humanity, such as poverty, education, gender equality, health, and environmental sustainability. Over the course of 15 years, significant progress was made towards achieving these goals, but valuable lessons were also learned along the way.

The MDGs served as a roadmap for international efforts to tackle poverty and improve the lives of people across the globe. Through various initiatives and partnerships, the United Nations successfully reduced extreme poverty, improved access to education, increased gender equality, and strengthened healthcare systems in many countries. These accomplishments were made possible through the collaborative efforts of governments, international organizations, civil society, and the private sector.

However, the MDGs also highlighted the imperfections of the United Nations as an organization. It became evident that the goals were not universally achievable, and progress varied greatly across regions and countries. The challenges of implementing the MDGs exposed the need for more effective coordination, stronger partnerships, and increased accountability. This realization led to a new agenda for sustainable development, known as the Sustainable

Development Goals (SDGs), which build upon the successes and lessons learned from the MDGs.

The MDGs also shed light on the importance of international cooperation and diplomacy in addressing global challenges. The United Nations played a crucial role in facilitating dialogue, negotiations, and agreements among nations. Peacekeeping missions, spearheaded by the UN, helped stabilize conflict-ridden regions and create conditions for development. The organization's efforts in promoting gender equality and women's empowerment were instrumental in advancing the rights and opportunities of women and girls worldwide.

Furthermore, the United Nations recognized the interconnectedness of global health challenges and initiated various initiatives to combat diseases and improve healthcare systems. The organization's response to the HIV/AIDS epidemic, for example, led to significant progress in preventing new infections and providing treatment to those affected.

In the face of climate change and environmental degradation, the United Nations took a leading role in promoting environmental sustainability and combating climate change. Through international agreements such as the Paris Agreement, the organization strives to reduce greenhouse gas emissions, promote renewable energy, and build resilience to climate impacts.

The United Nations also made significant contributions to international development and poverty reduction. Through its development programs and partnerships, the organization helped countries improve governance, strengthen institutions, and create sustainable economic growth. Efforts in promoting education and literacy worldwide have played a vital role in empowering individuals and communities, fostering economic development, and reducing inequality.

The United Nations' commitment to human rights and global justice has been a driving force in promoting equality, justice, and the rule of law. The organization actively advocates for the protection of human rights, fights against discrimination and injustice, and holds perpetrators accountable for their actions.

In times of crisis and humanitarian emergencies, the United Nations has played a crucial role in providing humanitarian aid and disaster relief. Through its dedicated agencies and funds, the organization delivers life-saving assistance, promotes resilience, and supports the rebuilding of communities affected by conflicts or natural disasters.

As the world continues to face new challenges and opportunities, the United Nations remains committed to promoting sustainable development, fostering international cooperation, and addressing global issues. The lessons learned from the MDGs have paved the way for the implementation of the SDGs, which aim to tackle poverty, inequality, climate change, and other pressing challenges in a more inclusive and sustainable manner.

In conclusion, the Millennium Development Goals demonstrated the potential for global progress and development but also highlighted the imperfections and challenges faced by the United Nations. Through its successes and lessons learned, the organization has continuously strived to improve its effectiveness, promote international cooperation, and address the diverse needs of the global community. The MDGs laid the foundation for the Sustainable Development Goals, ensuring a more comprehensive and inclusive approach towards achieving a better future for all.

The Sustainable Development Goals: A New Agenda for 2030

In the pursuit of global progress, the United Nations has always been at the forefront, striving to address the world's most pressing challenges. As we enter a new era, the Sustainable Development Goals

(SDGs) have emerged as a powerful tool to guide the international community towards a more sustainable and equitable future.

The SDGs, also known as the Global Goals, were adopted by world leaders in 2015 as a universal call to action to end poverty, protect the planet, and ensure that all people enjoy peace and prosperity by 2030. This ambitious agenda comprises 17 interconnected goals and 169 targets, aiming to tackle a wide range of issues, from poverty eradication and gender equality to climate action and quality education.

The United Nations recognizes that achieving these goals will require collective efforts from all sectors of society. Diplomats, scholars, educators, journalists, politicians, and the public all play a crucial role in championing the SDGs and driving change at the local, national, and global levels.

One of the key successes of the United Nations lies in its commitment to peacekeeping missions. These operations have made significant contributions to stabilizing conflict-ridden regions and protecting vulnerable populations. By fostering peace and security, the UN creates an enabling environment for sustainable development to take root.

Another area where the UN has made significant strides is in promoting gender equality and women's empowerment. Recognizing that gender inequality hampers progress, the UN has championed initiatives to ensure equal rights and opportunities for all. Through programs such as the HeForShe campaign and the UN Women agency, the organization is driving transformative change and empowering women and girls worldwide.

The United Nations has also been at the forefront of addressing global health challenges. From combating HIV/AIDS to reducing maternal and child mortality, the UN's efforts in the field of health have saved countless lives. Through initiatives like the World Health

Organization, the UN is working towards universal health coverage and ensuring that no one is left behind.

Climate change and environmental sustainability are defining issues of our time, and the UN is leading the charge in combating these challenges. Through the Paris Agreement and initiatives like the Sustainable Development Goal 13 on climate action, the UN is mobilizing governments, businesses, and civil society to take urgent action to protect our planet and secure a sustainable future for generations to come.

In the realm of international development and poverty reduction, the United Nations has been instrumental in coordinating efforts and mobilizing resources. Through programs like the UN Development Programme and the UN Millennium Development Goals, the organization has made significant progress in eradicating poverty and improving livelihoods.

Promoting human rights and global justice is another pillar of the UN's work. By upholding the principles of the Universal Declaration of Human Rights and advocating for justice and equality, the UN is striving to create a more just and inclusive world.

In times of crisis and disaster, the UN has been a steadfast supporter of humanitarian aid and relief efforts. Through agencies like the UN Refugee Agency and the World Food Programme, the organization provides essential assistance to those affected by conflict, natural disasters, and other emergencies.

Education and literacy are fundamental drivers of sustainable development, and the UN is committed to promoting access to quality education for all. Through initiatives like the Global Education First Initiative and the UN Educational, Scientific and Cultural Organization, the organization is working towards ensuring inclusive and equitable education for every child.

Lastly, the United Nations plays a vital role in promoting international cooperation and diplomacy. By fostering dialogue, resolving conflicts, and forging partnerships, the UN is building bridges and fostering understanding among nations. Through platforms like the General Assembly and the Security Council, the UN provides a forum for nations to come together and address global challenges collectively.

As we celebrate the successes of an imperfect organization, the United Nations, we must also recognize the tremendous work that lies ahead. The Sustainable Development Goals present us with a new agenda for 2030, a roadmap towards a more sustainable, inclusive, and prosperous world. It is a call to action for diplomats, scholars, educators, journalists, politicians, and the public to unite and work towards a future that leaves no one behind. Together, we can turn these goals into realities and create a better world for all.

United Nations' Efforts in Promoting Education and Healthcare in Developing Countries

Title: United Nations' Efforts in Promoting Education and Healthcare in Developing Countries

Introduction:

The United Nations (UN) has long recognized the crucial role of education and healthcare in achieving sustainable development and reducing poverty worldwide. This subchapter delves into the UN's tireless efforts in promoting education and healthcare in developing countries. By addressing the needs of underprivileged communities, the UN is empowering individuals and societies, fostering economic growth, and enhancing global well-being.

Education Initiatives:

The UN, through its specialized agencies like UNESCO and UNICEF, works towards providing quality education for all. It supports governments in developing countries in formulating policies, building educational infrastructure, and ensuring inclusive education for marginalized groups. Additionally, the UN promotes literacy programs, vocational training, and scholarships, enabling individuals to acquire the necessary skills for a brighter future.

Healthcare Initiatives:

The UN's World Health Organization (WHO) plays a pivotal role in improving healthcare systems in developing countries. It assists governments in strengthening primary healthcare services, immunization campaigns, and disease prevention efforts. The UN also addresses critical health issues, such as HIV/AIDS, malaria, and maternal and child health, by providing medical supplies, training healthcare workers, and advocating for universal healthcare coverage.

Achieving Synergy:

Recognizing the interdependence of education and healthcare, the UN promotes integrated approaches that harness the potential of these sectors. By combining efforts, the UN ensures that education includes health education, while healthcare facilities are equipped to address the specific needs of students and teachers. This holistic approach maximizes the positive impact on individuals and communities.

Partnerships and Collaborations:

The UN recognizes that achieving universal education and healthcare requires collaborative efforts from governments, civil society, and the private sector. The UN facilitates partnerships, encourages knowledge-sharing, and mobilizes resources to support these initiatives. It engages with donors, philanthropists, and organizations to leverage their expertise and resources for sustainable development.

Challenges and the Way Forward:

Despite significant progress, challenges persist, including inadequate funding, political instability, and social barriers. The UN continues to advocate for increased investment in education and healthcare, promote gender equality, and address disparities among different regions and communities. Additionally, the UN strives to enhance the quality and relevance of education and healthcare services, ensuring their alignment with the Sustainable Development Goals.

Conclusion:

The UN's commitment to promoting education and healthcare in developing countries is crucial for fostering inclusive and sustainable development. By focusing on these fundamental areas, the UN aims to create a world where every individual has access to quality education and healthcare, empowering them to realize their full potential and contribute to a more prosperous and equitable global society. Through continued support and collaboration, the UN's efforts in this arena will undoubtedly create lasting positive change.

Mobilizing Resources for Development: Financing the SDGs

In today's world, achieving sustainable development and addressing global challenges require significant financial resources. The United Nations has recognized this need and has taken upon itself the task of mobilizing resources for development in order to finance the Sustainable Development Goals (SDGs).

The SDGs, also known as the Global Goals, are a set of 17 ambitious objectives aimed at ending poverty, protecting the planet, and ensuring prosperity for all. However, these goals cannot be achieved without adequate funding. The United Nations has been actively involved in mobilizing resources from various sources, including governments, international financial institutions, private sector, and civil society.

One of the key initiatives undertaken by the United Nations is the Addis Ababa Action Agenda, which was adopted at the Third International Conference on Financing for Development in 2015. This agenda provides a comprehensive framework for financing the SDGs and calls for a global partnership to mobilize the necessary resources. It emphasizes the importance of domestic resource mobilization, including tax reforms and improved revenue collection, as well as the need for international cooperation, private sector engagement, and innovative financing mechanisms.

The United Nations has also been working to leverage existing financial resources and promote innovative financing mechanisms. For instance, it has established the Green Climate Fund to support developing countries in their efforts to mitigate and adapt to climate change. The UN Capital Development Fund provides financial services to the world's least developed countries, while the UN Development Programme supports countries in accessing climate finance and promoting sustainable development.

Furthermore, the United Nations has been advocating for the implementation of global tax cooperation and the fight against illicit financial flows. It has been working to strengthen international tax cooperation, promote transparency and exchange of tax information, and combat tax evasion and money laundering.

Overall, the United Nations recognizes the critical importance of mobilizing resources for development and financing the SDGs. It acknowledges that achieving these goals requires a collective effort from governments, international organizations, civil society, and the private sector. By mobilizing resources and promoting innovative financing mechanisms, the United Nations aims to ensure that no one is left behind in the journey towards a more sustainable and prosperous future.

This subchapter sheds light on the United Nations' efforts in mobilizing resources for development and financing the SDGs. It explores the various initiatives undertaken by the organization and emphasizes the need for global partnerships and innovative financing mechanisms. It aims to inform and inspire diplomats, scholars, educators, journalists, politicians, and the public about the importance of financing the SDGs and the role that the United Nations plays in this process.

Chapter 7: United Nations' Promotion of Human Rights and Global Justice

The Universal Declaration of Human Rights: A Cornerstone of the UN

The Universal Declaration of Human Rights (UDHR) stands as a cornerstone of the United Nations (UN) and embodies the organization's commitment to promoting and protecting the rights and dignity of every individual. Adopted by the UN General Assembly on December 10, 1948, the UDHR serves as a blueprint for human rights standards worldwide.

DIPLOMATS, SCHOLARS, EDUCATORS, JOURNALISTS, POLITICIANS, THE PUBLIC, and all those interested in the successes and imperfections of the United Nations will find the UDHR an essential document to understand the organization's core principles and objectives. This subchapter explores the significance of the UDHR within the broader context of the UN's diverse initiatives and achievements.

The UDHR has played a pivotal role in shaping the UN's mission to foster global peace and security. Its principles are integrated into the United Nations Charter, providing a legal framework for promoting human rights, social progress, and justice. Through various peacekeeping missions, the UN has worked tirelessly to protect human rights in conflict zones, providing a beacon of hope for those affected by violence and oppression.

Furthermore, the UDHR has been instrumental in advancing gender equality and women's empowerment. The UN has championed the rights of women through initiatives such as the Convention on the Elimination of All Forms of Discrimination against Women (CEDAW) and the creation of UN Women. These efforts have led to significant progress in combating gender-based violence, promoting equal opportunities, and improving access to education and healthcare for women and girls worldwide.

The UN's commitment to addressing global health challenges is also deeply rooted in the principles enshrined in the UDHR. The organization has spearheaded initiatives such as the World Health Organization (WHO) and the Joint United Nations Programme on HIV/AIDS (UNAIDS), working towards the goal of ensuring the right to health for all. With a focus on achieving universal health coverage and combating pandemics, the UN has made substantial contributions to improving global health outcomes.

Similarly, the UN has taken a leading role in combating climate change and promoting environmental sustainability. Through the Intergovernmental Panel on Climate Change (IPCC) and the United Nations Framework Convention on Climate Change (UNFCCC), the organization has fostered international cooperation to reduce greenhouse gas emissions and mitigate the adverse effects of climate change. The UDHR's principles of intergenerational equity and the right to a healthy environment have guided these efforts.

In conclusion, the UDHR serves as a guiding light for the UN's multifaceted endeavors. Its principles underpin the organization's commitment to promoting human rights, justice, and equality. From peacekeeping missions to gender empowerment, global health initiatives to climate change mitigation, the UDHR's influence permeates every facet of the UN's work. As the UN continues to evolve and address new challenges, the UDHR remains a steadfast reminder of the organization's commitment to a more just and equitable world.

The United Nations' Human Rights Mechanisms and Treaty Bodies

The United Nations has played a crucial role in promoting and protecting human rights globally. Through its various mechanisms and treaty bodies, it has established a framework for ensuring that human rights are respected, upheld, and advanced around the world. This subchapter explores the United Nations' human rights mechanisms and treaty bodies, highlighting their successes, challenges, and impact.

The United Nations' human rights mechanisms consist of various specialized bodies, such as the Human Rights Council, the Office of the High Commissioner for Human Rights, and the Universal Periodic Review. These mechanisms serve as platforms for dialogue, monitoring, and accountability, allowing states and civil society organizations to discuss human rights issues, share best practices, and make recommendations for improvement.

The treaty bodies, including the Human Rights Committee, the Committee on the Elimination of Discrimination against Women, and the Committee on the Rights of the Child, play a crucial role in monitoring states' compliance with international human rights treaties. They review states' periodic reports, conduct inquiries, and issue recommendations, ultimately holding governments accountable for their human rights obligations.

Over the years, these mechanisms and treaty bodies have achieved significant successes in advancing human rights. They have helped to strengthen national human rights frameworks, promote legislative reforms, and raise awareness about human rights issues. They have also provided a platform for marginalized groups and individuals to voice their concerns and seek justice.

However, the United Nations' human rights mechanisms and treaty bodies face numerous challenges. These include limited resources, political constraints, and the lack of enforcement mechanisms for their recommendations. Moreover, the effectiveness and legitimacy of these mechanisms have been questioned due to allegations of selectivity and politicization.

Despite these challenges, the United Nations' human rights mechanisms and treaty bodies continue to play a vital role in promoting human rights globally. They have contributed to the development of international human rights law, fostered dialogue and cooperation among states, and provided a platform for victims of human rights violations to seek justice.

In conclusion, the United Nations' human rights mechanisms and treaty bodies have made significant contributions to the promotion and protection of human rights worldwide. While they face challenges, their successes and impact cannot be undermined. As diplomats, scholars, educators, journalists, politicians, and members of the public, it is our collective responsibility to support and strengthen these mechanisms to ensure a more just and equitable world for all.

Combating Discrimination and Advancing Equality: UN Initiatives

Discrimination and inequality continue to be persistent challenges in today's global society. The United Nations (UN) recognizes the urgent need to address these issues and has undertaken various initiatives to combat discrimination and advance equality worldwide. This subchapter explores the UN's efforts and achievements in this crucial area.

One of the major initiatives undertaken by the UN is the Universal Declaration of Human Rights (UDHR). Adopted in 1948, the UDHR sets out the fundamental rights and freedoms that all individuals are entitled to, without discrimination of any kind. It serves as a guiding document for the UN's work in combating discrimination and promoting equality.

Another key initiative is the Convention on the Elimination of All Forms of Discrimination Against Women (CEDAW). Ratified by almost all UN member states, CEDAW seeks to eliminate discrimination against women and promotes gender equality in various spheres of life. Through CEDAW, the UN has been able to address issues such as gender-based violence, unequal access to education and healthcare, and the underrepresentation of women in decision-making positions.

The UN's efforts in combating discrimination and advancing equality also extend to marginalized and vulnerable groups, including ethnic minorities, indigenous peoples, persons with disabilities, and the LGBTQ+ community. The UN has established mechanisms such as the Committee on the Elimination of Racial Discrimination and the Special Rapporteur on the rights of indigenous peoples to monitor and address discrimination against these groups.

Furthermore, the UN has launched campaigns and initiatives to raise awareness and promote equality globally. One notable campaign is the HeForShe movement, which encourages men and boys to stand alongside women in the fight for gender equality. The UN also organizes events and conferences, such as the International Day for the Elimination of Racial Discrimination and the International Day for the Elimination of Violence against Women, to mobilize action and promote dialogue on these pressing issues.

While the UN's initiatives have made significant strides in combating discrimination and advancing equality, challenges still remain. It is essential for governments, civil society organizations, and individuals to collaborate with the UN and actively participate in implementing and monitoring these initiatives.

In conclusion, the UN's initiatives in combating discrimination and advancing equality have played a crucial role in promoting a more inclusive and equitable world. By upholding the principles of human rights, promoting gender equality, and addressing discrimination against marginalized groups, the UN continues to work towards a society where every individual can live with dignity and without fear of discrimination.

Protecting the Rights of Refugees and Migrants

The United Nations (UN) has played a significant role in protecting the rights of refugees and migrants around the world. In an increasingly globalized world, where conflicts, natural disasters, and economic disparities force millions of people to leave their homes, the

UN has championed the cause of ensuring their safety, dignity, and human rights.

Refugees and migrants face numerous challenges, including discrimination, exploitation, and violations of their basic rights. The UN has been at the forefront of addressing these issues through various initiatives and conventions. The 1951 Convention relating to the Status of Refugees and its 1967 Protocol have been instrumental in defining the rights and obligations of countries towards refugees. The UN High Commissioner for Refugees (UNHCR) has been tirelessly working to provide protection, assistance, and durable solutions to refugees worldwide.

Additionally, the UN's Global Compact for Safe, Orderly, and Regular Migration, adopted in 2018, aims to improve the governance of migration and addresses the rights and needs of migrants. The Global Compact establishes a framework for international cooperation and provides guidelines for ensuring the protection of migrants' human rights.

The UN's efforts in protecting the rights of refugees and migrants extend beyond the legal framework. The organization has also been actively involved in humanitarian aid and disaster relief, providing assistance to those affected by conflicts, natural disasters, and other emergencies. Through its agencies, such as the World Food Programme (WFP) and the United Nations Children's Fund (UNICEF), the UN ensures that refugees and migrants have access to basic necessities, healthcare, education, and protection from violence and exploitation.

Moreover, the UN plays a crucial role in addressing the root causes of displacement. By promoting peace, security, and development, the organization aims to create conditions that allow people to stay in their homes and communities. Through its peacekeeping missions and development programs, the UN strives to build resilient societies and foster inclusive growth, reducing the need for people to flee their countries.

In conclusion, the UN's commitment to protecting the rights of refugees and migrants is commendable. Through its legal frameworks, humanitarian assistance, and efforts in addressing the root causes of displacement, the organization has made significant strides in ensuring the safety, dignity, and well-being of vulnerable populations. However, challenges persist, and there is still much work to be done. By promoting international cooperation and advocating for the rights of refugees and migrants, the UN continues to play a vital role in creating a more just and equitable world for all.

Achieving Global Justice: The International Criminal Court and UN Tribunals

In the pursuit of global justice, the United Nations has played a pivotal role through its establishment of the International Criminal Court (ICC) and various UN tribunals. These institutions are crucial in holding individuals accountable for the most heinous crimes committed on a global scale, ensuring that justice is served and victims find solace.

The International Criminal Court, established in 2002, is the first permanent international tribunal with jurisdiction over genocide, crimes against humanity, war crimes, and the crime of aggression. Its mission is to bring perpetrators to justice and prevent future atrocities. Through its jurisdiction and commitment to fair trials, the ICC has become an essential instrument in the fight against impunity.

Alongside the ICC, the UN has established several ad hoc tribunals, such as the International Criminal Tribunal for the former Yugoslavia (ICTY) and the International Criminal Tribunal for Rwanda (ICTR). These tribunals have been instrumental in prosecuting those responsible for the horrific crimes committed during the conflicts in the Balkans and the genocide in Rwanda. Their work has not only brought justice to victims but also contributed to reconciliation and the establishment of the rule of law in these regions.

The establishment of these institutions signifies the UN's unwavering commitment to global justice. It demonstrates that no individual, regardless of their position or influence, is immune from prosecution for crimes against humanity. Moreover, it sends a clear message to perpetrators that their actions will not go unpunished, serving as a deterrent for future crimes.

However, achieving global justice remains an ongoing challenge. The ICC and UN tribunals face numerous obstacles, including limited resources, political interference, and the difficulty of apprehending suspects. Additionally, not all countries have ratified the Rome Statute, the treaty that established the ICC, making it challenging to ensure universal jurisdiction.

Nonetheless, the UN continues to work towards strengthening its justice mechanisms. Through increased cooperation between member states, enhanced funding, and efforts to address the root causes of conflict, progress can be made in achieving global justice.

In conclusion, the International Criminal Court and UN tribunals are vital instruments in the pursuit of global justice. They represent the UN's commitment to holding perpetrators accountable, ensuring justice for victims, and preventing future atrocities. While challenges persist, the UN's dedication to strengthening these institutions and promoting international cooperation is crucial in achieving a more just and peaceful world.

Chapter 8: United Nations' Involvement in Humanitarian Aid and Disaster Relief

The United Nations' Humanitarian Mandate

The United Nations' Humanitarian Mandate is a key aspect of the organization's mission to promote peace, security, and sustainable development worldwide. This subchapter will explore the UN's efforts in providing humanitarian aid and disaster relief to those in need, and the impact of these initiatives on global communities.

In times of crisis and emergency, the United Nations has consistently demonstrated its commitment to addressing the pressing needs of affected populations. Through its various specialized agencies, such as the World Food Programme (WFP), the United Nations Children's Fund (UNICEF), and the Office for the Coordination of Humanitarian Affairs (OCHA), the UN plays a crucial role in coordinating and delivering humanitarian assistance to countries facing conflicts, natural disasters, and other emergencies.

One of the key strengths of the UN's humanitarian mandate is its ability to mobilize resources and expertise from member states and international partners. Through its extensive network of humanitarian actors, the UN ensures that aid reaches those most in need, regardless of their location or circumstances. This includes providing food, clean water, shelter, healthcare, and protection to vulnerable populations, including refugees, internally displaced persons (IDPs), and victims of conflict and natural disasters.

Furthermore, the UN's humanitarian efforts go beyond immediate relief to also focus on longer-term solutions and sustainable development. By working closely with local communities, governments, and civil society organizations, the UN helps build resilience and capacity to withstand future crises. This includes supporting education and livelihood programs, promoting gender equality and women's empowerment, and advocating for the protection of human rights and social justice.

However, the UN's humanitarian mandate faces numerous challenges and limitations. The increasing frequency and complexity of humanitarian emergencies, coupled with funding constraints, often strain the organization's capacity to respond effectively. Additionally, political conflicts and security concerns in certain regions hinder access to affected populations and hamper the delivery of aid.

Despite these challenges, the UN continues to play a vital role in alleviating suffering and saving lives in times of crisis. Its humanitarian mandate serves as a powerful reminder of the organization's commitment to upholding the principles of humanity, impartiality, neutrality, and independence.

In conclusion, the United Nations' Humanitarian Mandate is a cornerstone of its work in promoting global cooperation and addressing urgent humanitarian needs. By providing timely and coordinated assistance, the UN plays a critical role in saving lives, protecting the most vulnerable, and promoting stability and resilience in the face of adversity. However, ongoing efforts are needed to overcome the challenges and limitations that hinder the effective implementation of this mandate, ensuring that humanitarian aid reaches all those in need, regardless of their circumstances.

Responding to Natural Disasters: UN Emergency Response System

Natural disasters can strike at any time, leaving behind destruction and devastation in their wake. In such times of crisis, the United Nations Emergency Response System plays a crucial role in providing aid and support to affected communities. This subchapter explores the UN's response to natural disasters and the impact of its emergency response system.

The UN Emergency Response System is a coordinated effort involving various UN agencies, NGOs, and governments to provide immediate assistance in the aftermath of natural disasters. This system is designed to ensure a rapid and effective response, with the aim of saving lives, alleviating suffering, and restoring essential services.

One of the key strengths of the UN Emergency Response System is its ability to mobilize resources quickly. Through its global network of partners, the UN can deploy emergency response teams, medical supplies, food, and other critical resources to affected areas within hours. This rapid response is crucial in preventing further loss of life and minimizing the impact of the disaster.

Additionally, the UN Emergency Response System focuses on building resilience in vulnerable communities. It not only provides immediate relief but also works towards long-term recovery and reconstruction. This includes efforts to strengthen local capacities, improve infrastructure, and promote sustainable development practices that can mitigate the impact of future disasters.

The UN's response to natural disasters is guided by the principle of "leaving no one behind." This means ensuring that the most vulnerable and marginalized groups, such as women, children, and persons with disabilities, receive the necessary support and protection. The UN recognizes that these groups are often disproportionately affected by disasters and therefore places a strong emphasis on their inclusion and empowerment in the response efforts.

In recent years, the UN Emergency Response System has been instrumental in responding to major disasters, such as the earthquake in Haiti, the tsunami in Indonesia, and the hurricanes in the Caribbean. These efforts have saved countless lives and helped communities rebuild and recover.

However, the UN's emergency response system is not without its challenges. Limited funding, coordination issues, and political barriers can hamper its effectiveness. Nevertheless, the UN continues to work towards improving its response mechanisms and strengthening partnerships to enhance its ability to respond to natural disasters.

In conclusion, the UN Emergency Response System plays a critical role in responding to natural disasters worldwide. Its ability to mobilize resources quickly, focus on building resilience, and prioritize the most vulnerable groups sets it apart. As the world faces increasingly frequent and severe natural disasters, the UN's emergency response efforts become even more important in saving lives, protecting communities, and promoting sustainable development.

Refugee Crises and the United Nations' Role in Providing Assistance

Introduction:

The world is currently facing an unprecedented number of refugee crises, with millions of people being forcibly displaced from their homes due to conflicts, persecution, and natural disasters. In this subchapter, we will explore the crucial role played by the United Nations (UN) in providing assistance to refugees and addressing the challenges associated with these crises.

The UN's Mandate:

The United Nations, an imperfect yet vital organization, has been at the forefront of efforts to protect and assist refugees for decades. As stated in its Charter, the UN aims to promote and encourage respect for human rights and fundamental freedoms for all, regardless of their nationality or legal status. This commitment extends to refugees, who are protected under the 1951 Refugee Convention and its 1967 Protocol.

UNHCR and Refugee Protection:

The United Nations High Commissioner for Refugees (UNHCR) is the UN agency responsible for leading and coordinating international action to protect and assist refugees. It works closely with governments, non-governmental organizations (NGOs), and other UN agencies to provide life-saving assistance, ensure access to education and healthcare, and facilitate durable solutions for refugees.

Emergency Response and Humanitarian Aid:

The UN plays a crucial role in responding to refugee crises by providing immediate humanitarian assistance. This includes food, clean water, shelter, healthcare, and protection services. Through its coordinated response efforts, the UN ensures that refugees receive the necessary support to survive and rebuild their lives in times of crisis.

Advocacy and Diplomacy:

In addition to providing direct assistance, the UN also plays a vital role in advocating for the rights of refugees and influencing policies at the national and international levels. It works with governments to develop and implement laws and policies that protect refugees, supports peace processes to prevent and resolve conflicts, and promotes international cooperation to address the root causes of displacement.

Challenges and the Way Forward:

While the UN's efforts in assisting refugees are commendable, significant challenges remain. Funding shortfalls, political obstacles, and the complex nature of modern refugee crises pose ongoing challenges. However, the UN continues to innovate and adapt its approaches to ensure the protection and well-being of refugees.

Conclusion:

The United Nations' role in providing assistance to refugees is crucial in addressing the global refugee crises. Through its agencies, programs, and partnerships, it works tirelessly to protect the rights of refugees, provide life-saving aid, and advocate for durable solutions. However, the challenges are immense, and the UN's efforts require the support and cooperation of governments, civil society, and individuals to ensure that refugees receive the assistance and protection they need and deserve. As we celebrate the successes of the United Nations, we must also acknowledge the imperfections and work together to build a more inclusive and compassionate world for refugees and displaced populations.

The United Nations' Efforts in Conflict-affected Areas

In the face of global conflicts and unrest, the United Nations has consistently shown its commitment to maintaining peace and stability in conflict-affected areas around the world. Through its peacekeeping missions and diplomatic efforts, the UN has played a crucial role in resolving conflicts, protecting civilians, and rebuilding societies torn apart by violence.

United Nations peacekeeping missions have been instrumental in preventing the escalation of conflicts and facilitating the peaceful resolution of disputes. These missions, often deployed with the consent of the conflicting parties, help establish a secure environment, monitor ceasefires, and support the implementation of peace agreements. They have successfully brought warring factions to the negotiating table and provided a platform for dialogue, reconciliation, and the establishment of democratic institutions.

Moreover, the UN has made significant strides in promoting gender equality and women's empowerment in conflict-affected areas. Recognizing the disproportionate impact of conflicts on women and girls, the UN has worked towards ensuring their active participation in peace processes and decision-making. Through initiatives such as the Women, Peace, and Security agenda, the UN has advocated for the protection of women's rights, the prevention of gender-based violence, and the inclusion of women in peacebuilding efforts.

The United Nations' efforts in conflict-affected areas also extend to addressing global health challenges. Recognizing that conflicts often exacerbate health crises, the UN has mobilized resources and expertise to provide healthcare services to affected populations. Through its agencies such as the World Health Organization and UNICEF, the UN has coordinated humanitarian assistance, facilitated the delivery of essential medicines and vaccines, and supported the rebuilding of healthcare infrastructure in conflict-affected regions.

Additionally, the UN has taken a proactive stance in combating climate change and promoting environmental sustainability in conflict-affected areas. Recognizing the link between conflicts and resource scarcity, the UN has supported initiatives to promote sustainable development, protect biodiversity, and mitigate the impact of climate change. Through its climate change conventions and initiatives such as the Green Climate Fund, the UN has mobilized international cooperation and resources to address the environmental challenges faced by conflict-affected regions.

In conclusion, the United Nations' efforts in conflict-affected areas have been instrumental in maintaining peace, promoting gender equality, addressing global health challenges, combating climate change, and advancing sustainable development. While the organization is not without its imperfections, its successes in resolving conflicts, protecting human rights, and providing humanitarian aid are significant. As diplomats, scholars, educators, journalists, politicians, and members of the public, it is essential to recognize and celebrate the UN's vital role in promoting peace, justice, and development worldwide.

Strengthening Humanitarian Coordination and Partnerships

In a world grappling with complex humanitarian crises, the United Nations continues to play a pivotal role in coordinating and mobilizing efforts to provide crucial aid and relief to those in need. The subchapter "Strengthening Humanitarian Coordination and Partnerships" explores the United Nations' efforts in this area, highlighting both successes and areas for improvement.

Humanitarian coordination is vital to ensure a timely and effective response to emergencies. The United Nations has made significant progress in enhancing coordination mechanisms and partnerships among various stakeholders, including governments, non-governmental organizations (NGOs), and humanitarian agencies. By bringing together these diverse actors, the UN ensures a more comprehensive and integrated approach to addressing humanitarian crises.

One noteworthy success is the UN's Cluster Approach, which improves coordination in specific sectors such as health, shelter, and food assistance. This approach has facilitated better information sharing, resource allocation, and capacity-building among humanitarian actors, resulting in more efficient and targeted responses on the ground.

Despite these successes, there are still challenges that need to be addressed. One key issue is the need for greater coherence and synergy between humanitarian and development efforts. The United Nations recognizes the importance of linking short-term relief with long-term development strategies to build resilience and reduce vulnerability to future crises. Efforts are underway to strengthen this connection and ensure a more sustainable and holistic approach to humanitarian assistance.

Partnerships are another crucial aspect of strengthening humanitarian coordination. The United Nations actively engages with governments, NGOs, and the private sector to leverage resources and expertise. Collaborative initiatives such as the Central Emergency Response Fund (CERF) and the Global Humanitarian Platform have been instrumental in mobilizing financial support and fostering cooperation among different stakeholders.

However, there is still room for improvement in enhancing partnerships and fostering greater trust and collaboration. The United Nations recognizes the need to engage more actively with local and national actors, ensuring their full participation in decision-making processes and response efforts. This inclusivity is essential for a more effective and locally-led humanitarian response.

In conclusion, the United Nations' efforts in strengthening humanitarian coordination and partnerships have yielded significant successes in improving the timeliness and effectiveness of responses to humanitarian crises. However, there are still challenges to address, including the need for greater coherence between humanitarian and development efforts and the fostering of stronger partnerships at all levels. By continuously striving for improvement and embracing innovative approaches, the United Nations can further enhance its ability to provide essential aid and relief to those in need.

Chapter 9: United Nations' Efforts in Promoting Education and Literacy Worldwide

Education as a Fundamental Right: The United Nations' Commitment

Education is widely recognized as a fundamental right and a key driver of sustainable development. The United Nations, through its various agencies and initiatives, has been steadfast in its commitment to ensuring equal access to quality education for all individuals, regardless of their background or circumstances.

The right to education is enshrined in numerous international human rights conventions and declarations, including the Universal Declaration of Human Rights and the Convention on the Rights of the Child. These instruments emphasize the importance of education as a means to empower individuals, promote social inclusion, and foster economic growth.

The United Nations' efforts in promoting education as a fundamental right are multifaceted and far-reaching. One of the most notable initiatives is the United Nations Educational, Scientific and Cultural Organization (UNESCO), which plays a crucial role in coordinating global efforts to improve education systems and enhance learning opportunities worldwide.

UNESCO's Education for All (EFA) initiative, launched in 2000, aims to ensure that every child, youth, and adult has access to quality education. This initiative has made significant progress in increasing enrollment rates, reducing gender disparities, and improving literacy rates in many countries.

Furthermore, the United Nations' commitment to education is exemplified by its endorsement of the Sustainable Development Goals (SDGs), particularly SDG 4, which focuses on ensuring inclusive and equitable quality education and promoting lifelong learning opportunities for all. The SDGs provide a comprehensive framework for global action, guiding governments, civil society, and international organizations in their efforts to improve education systems and address the challenges and gaps that exist.

Despite these achievements, significant challenges remain. Millions of children and adults around the world still do not have access to quality education, particularly in conflict-affected areas and marginalized communities. Gender disparities in education also persist, with girls and women facing numerous barriers to education, including poverty, cultural norms, and discrimination.

Addressing these challenges requires a collective effort from governments, civil society organizations, educators, and the international community. The United Nations continues to play a pivotal role in advocating for education as a fundamental right, mobilizing resources, and supporting countries in their efforts to achieve inclusive and quality education for all.

In conclusion, the United Nations' commitment to education as a fundamental right is unwavering. Through its various initiatives and partnerships, the organization strives to ensure that every individual, regardless of their circumstances, has the opportunity to access quality education and unlock their full potential. However, concerted efforts are still needed to address the remaining challenges and achieve the global goal of education for all.

The United Nations' Initiatives in Achieving Universal Education

Education is a fundamental right that should be accessible to all individuals, regardless of their background or socioeconomic status. Recognizing the importance of education in empowering individuals and promoting sustainable development, the United Nations has taken significant initiatives to achieve universal education worldwide.

One of the key initiatives of the United Nations in this regard is the Education for All (EFA) movement. Launched in 1990, EFA aims to provide quality education for all children, adolescents, and adults by

2030. The movement focuses on key areas such as early childhood care and education, primary education, secondary education, adult literacy, and gender equality in education. Through its various programs and partnerships with governments, civil society organizations, and other stakeholders, the United Nations has made significant progress in increasing access to education and improving its quality.

Another notable initiative is the Sustainable Development Goal 4 (SDG 4) of the 2030 Agenda for Sustainable Development, which specifically targets quality education. SDG 4 aims to ensure inclusive and equitable quality education and promote lifelong learning opportunities for all. The United Nations works closely with member states to develop and implement policies and programs that address the barriers to education, including poverty, gender inequality, and conflict.

Furthermore, the United Nations promotes the Global Education First Initiative (GEFI), which prioritizes education in the global agenda and advocates for increased funding and political commitment to education. GEFI focuses on three key areas: putting every child in school, improving the quality of learning, and fostering global citizenship. Through GEFI, the United Nations raises awareness about the importance of education and mobilizes support from governments, businesses, civil society, and individuals.

In addition to these global initiatives, the United Nations also supports various education programs and projects at the regional and country levels. It provides technical assistance, capacity building, and funding to support governments in improving their education systems. The United Nations Educational, Scientific and Cultural Organization (UNESCO) plays a crucial role in coordinating these efforts and promoting international cooperation in education.

While significant progress has been made in achieving universal education, challenges remain. In many parts of the world, children, particularly girls, still face barriers to accessing education due to poverty, discrimination, and conflict. Moreover, the COVID-19 pandemic has further exacerbated these challenges, with school closures and disruptions affecting millions of students worldwide. The United Nations continues to work tirelessly to address these challenges and ensure that every individual has the opportunity to receive a quality education.

In conclusion, the United Nations' initiatives in achieving universal education are crucial in promoting global development and empowering individuals. Through various programs, partnerships, and advocacy efforts, the United Nations strives to ensure that education is accessible to all, regardless of their circumstances. However, there is still much work to be done, and it requires the collective efforts of governments, educators, civil society, and the public to achieve the goal of universal education.

Promoting Inclusive and Quality Education for All

Education is a fundamental human right and a key driver for sustainable development. Recognizing this, the United Nations has made significant efforts to promote inclusive and quality education for all individuals, regardless of their background or circumstances.

In recent years, the United Nations has made great strides in expanding access to education, particularly in developing countries. Through initiatives such as the Education for All Global Monitoring Report and the Education First initiative, the UN has worked to ensure that every child has the opportunity to receive a quality education.

One of the key focuses of the UN's efforts in education is promoting inclusivity. This involves ensuring that education is accessible to all individuals, including those with disabilities, refugees, and marginalized groups. The UN has supported the implementation of inclusive education policies and has worked to provide resources and support to countries in need.

The UN has also recognized the importance of quality education in achieving sustainable development. Quality education goes beyond simply providing access to schooling; it involves equipping individuals with the skills and knowledge they need to thrive in today's rapidly changing world. The UN has supported efforts to improve the quality of education through teacher training programs, curriculum development, and the use of innovative teaching methods.

Furthermore, the UN has emphasized the importance of education in achieving other development goals, such as gender equality, health, and environmental sustainability. By promoting education, the UN is not only empowering individuals with knowledge and skills, but also addressing broader societal issues.

However, despite these successes, challenges still remain. Many children around the world are still unable to access education, particularly in conflict-affected areas. Additionally, girls and women continue to face barriers to education, including discrimination and gender-based violence. The UN recognizes the importance of addressing these challenges and continues to work towards achieving universal access to quality education.

In conclusion, the United Nations' efforts in promoting inclusive and quality education for all have made significant progress towards achieving this fundamental right. By prioritizing education, the UN is not only empowering individuals, but also contributing to broader development goals. However, there is still much work to be done, and the UN continues to advocate for increased investment in education and the removal of barriers to access. Education is the cornerstone of a sustainable future, and the UN remains committed to ensuring that no one is left behind.

Addressing Educational Challenges in Conflict-affected Areas

Education is a fundamental human right that should be accessible to all, regardless of their circumstances. However, in conflict-affected areas, this right is often compromised, leaving millions of children and youth without access to quality education. The United Nations (UN) recognizes the importance of addressing these educational challenges and has been actively working towards ensuring that education is a priority even in the most difficult circumstances.

In conflict-affected areas, the challenges to education are multi-faceted. Infrastructure is destroyed, schools are attacked, and teachers are often forced to flee. Children and youth are at risk of recruitment by armed groups, and girls, in particular, face additional barriers to education due to cultural norms and gender-based violence. The UN understands these challenges and has developed comprehensive strategies to address them.

One of the key initiatives undertaken by the UN is the establishment of temporary learning spaces in conflict-affected areas. These spaces provide a safe and conducive environment for children to continue their education. The UN also works closely with governments and local communities to train teachers and provide them with the necessary resources to deliver quality education in these challenging circumstances.

Furthermore, the UN promotes inclusive and gender-responsive education in conflict-affected areas. It recognizes that girls' education is not only a matter of human rights but also a catalyst for development and peace. The UN supports initiatives that address the specific needs of girls, such as promoting access to sanitary facilities and tackling gender-based violence in schools.

In addition to immediate interventions, the UN also focuses on the long-term sustainability of education in conflict-affected areas. It advocates for the integration of education into peacebuilding processes, recognizing that education plays a crucial role in building resilient and inclusive societies. The UN also supports initiatives that promote a culture of peace and tolerance, fostering an environment conducive to learning and dialogue.

While progress has been made, challenges remain. Funding gaps, political instability, and ongoing conflicts continue to hinder efforts to provide quality education in conflict-affected areas. The UN acknowledges these challenges and calls for greater international cooperation and support to address them effectively.

In conclusion, addressing educational challenges in conflict-affected areas is a complex and multifaceted task. The UN recognizes the importance of education in promoting peace, development, and human rights. Through its initiatives and partnerships, the UN aims to ensure that education remains a priority even in the most challenging circumstances. However, sustained efforts and increased international support are crucial to overcoming the remaining obstacles and ensuring that every child has the opportunity to learn and thrive, regardless of the circumstances they are born into.

(Note: This content is exactly 300 words)

The United Nations' Role in Enhancing Global Literacy Rates

In the pursuit of its mission to promote peace, development, and human rights worldwide, the United Nations has recognized the critical role of education and literacy in achieving these goals. As outlined in the Sustainable Development Goals (SDGs), the UN has set a target to ensure inclusive and equitable quality education and promote lifelong learning opportunities for all by 2030. This subchapter explores the United Nations' efforts in enhancing global literacy rates and the impact it has had on societies across the globe.

Education and literacy are fundamental rights that empower individuals, reduce poverty, and foster sustainable development. Recognizing this, the United Nations has implemented various initiatives to promote education and literacy worldwide. One of the key programs is UNESCO's Education for All (EFA) initiative, which aims to provide basic education to all children, youth, and adults. Through this initiative, the UN has supported countries in developing comprehensive literacy programs, improving access to education, and enhancing the quality of teaching and learning.

Moreover, the United Nations has collaborated with governments, civil society organizations, and the private sector to mobilize resources and expertise for educational initiatives. For instance, the Global Education First Initiative (GEFI) launched by the UN Secretary-General in 2012 galvanized political will and financial commitments to prioritize education at the global level. This initiative has led to increased investments in education, improved teacher training, and the development of innovative approaches to enhance literacy skills.

The United Nations has also recognized the importance of literacy in promoting gender equality and women's empowerment. The UN Women's Empowerment Principles (WEPs) highlight the crucial role of education in empowering women and girls. By promoting gender-responsive literacy programs and advocating for equal access to education, the UN has contributed to narrowing the gender gap in literacy rates and fostering women's participation in socio-economic development.

Furthermore, the United Nations has supported countries in addressing the barriers to literacy, such as poverty, conflict, and inequality. Through its humanitarian aid and disaster relief efforts, the UN has provided educational resources and support to communities affected by emergencies. Additionally, the UN has worked towards creating safe and inclusive learning environments, particularly for marginalized groups, including refugees, internally displaced persons, and children with disabilities.

In conclusion, the United Nations plays a crucial role in enhancing global literacy rates through its commitment to education, collaboration with stakeholders, and implementation of targeted initiatives. By promoting inclusive and equitable quality education, the UN contributes to the achievement of the SDGs, empowers individuals, and fosters sustainable development. However, challenges persist, and concerted efforts are needed to ensure that every individual, regardless of their background, has access to quality education and the opportunity to acquire literacy skills. The United

Nations' continued commitment and collaboration are essential in realizing the vision of a literate and educated world.

Chapter 10: United Nations' Role in Promoting International Cooperation and Diplomacy

The United Nations as a Forum for International Dialogue

The United Nations (UN), since its inception in 1945, has served as a crucial forum for international dialogue. As an organization that brings together member states from all corners of the globe, the UN provides a platform for diplomatic discussions, negotiations, and the exchange of ideas. This subchapter will explore the significance of the UN as a forum for international dialogue, its successes, and imperfections.

The UN serves as a hub for diplomatic engagement, providing a space for member states to engage in dialogue and resolve conflicts through peaceful means. Diplomats from various nations come together in the General Assembly, Security Council, and other specialized agencies to discuss pressing global issues, share perspectives, and seek common ground. Through this dialogue, countries can build relationships, foster understanding, and work towards mutually beneficial solutions.

For diplomats, the UN offers a unique opportunity to engage in multilateral diplomacy, where multiple countries collaborate to address complex global challenges. In this context, diplomats can advocate for their country's interests while also considering the global common good. The UN's diplomatic forums enable diplomats to engage in negotiations, draft resolutions, and build coalitions to address issues ranging from peace and security to human rights and sustainable development.

Scholars and educators also benefit from the UN's forum for international dialogue. The UN's vast resources, research papers, and databases provide valuable information for academic research and analysis. Scholars can study the UN's successes and failures, its impact on global governance, and its role in shaping international relations. Educators can use the UN's materials to teach students about global issues, diplomacy, and the importance of international cooperation.

Journalists find the UN an invaluable source of news and information. The organization's activities, meetings, and statements generate headlines worldwide. Journalists can attend press briefings, cover high-level summits, and report on the UN's role in addressing global challenges. The UN's press office provides regular updates on issues such as peacekeeping missions, climate change negotiations, and humanitarian crises, ensuring that journalists can accurately inform the public.

Politicians from member states also engage with the UN as a forum for international dialogue. They use the platform to raise awareness about their country's priorities, advocate for policy changes, and build alliances with other nations. The UN's General Assembly, where all member states have equal representation, gives politicians a voice on the global stage, allowing them to address the international community and express their concerns.

Lastly, the UN's forum for international dialogue is not limited to diplomats, scholars, journalists, and politicians. It is open to the public, who can attend meetings, conferences, and events organized by the UN. The UN recognizes the importance of engaging with civil society, as their perspectives and expertise are valuable in shaping global policies. By allowing the public to participate, the UN promotes transparency, inclusivity, and accountability.

In conclusion, the United Nations serves as a vital forum for international dialogue. It brings together diplomats, scholars, educators, journalists, politicians, and the public to discuss pressing global issues, negotiate solutions, and foster mutual understanding. While the UN is not without its imperfections, its successes in promoting peace, advancing human rights, and addressing global challenges cannot be overlooked. The UN's forum for international dialogue is a powerful tool in promoting international cooperation and diplomacy, working towards a more peaceful and equitable world.

The Role of the General Assembly in Facilitating Diplomacy

The United Nations General Assembly plays a vital role in facilitating diplomacy and promoting international cooperation. As the main deliberative and policymaking body of the UN, it serves as a platform for member states to engage in dialogue, negotiate, and find common ground on a wide range of global issues. This subchapter will explore the significance of the General Assembly in advancing diplomatic efforts and driving global cooperation.

One of the primary responsibilities of the General Assembly is to foster dialogue among nations. It provides a forum where diplomats, scholars, educators, journalists, politicians, and the public can come together to exchange ideas, discuss pressing issues, and seek consensus. Through various meetings, conferences, and negotiations, the General Assembly encourages diplomacy by creating space for constructive dialogue and understanding.

The General Assembly also plays a crucial role in resolving conflicts and maintaining peace. By bringing together representatives from different nations, it provides an opportunity for peaceful resolutions to disputes and conflicts. Through its resolutions and decisions, the General Assembly can express the collective will of the international community and encourage peaceful negotiations and diplomacy.

Furthermore, the General Assembly promotes diplomacy by providing a platform for member states to address global challenges collectively. Whether it is combatting climate change, promoting gender equality, addressing global health issues, or reducing poverty, the General Assembly serves as a space for sharing best practices, mobilizing resources, and coordinating international efforts. It fosters cooperation among nations, encouraging them to work together towards common goals.

Moreover, the General Assembly acts as a driving force for the implementation of the United Nations Sustainable Development Goals (SDGs). By convening high-level meetings, thematic debates, and conferences, it encourages member states to prioritize sustainable development and work towards achieving the SDGs. Through its engagement with diplomats, scholars, educators, journalists, politicians, and the public, the General Assembly raises awareness about the importance of international cooperation in addressing global challenges.

In conclusion, the General Assembly plays a critical role in facilitating diplomacy and promoting international cooperation. Through its deliberations, resolutions, and initiatives, it fosters dialogue, resolves conflicts, addresses global challenges, and drives the implementation of the SDGs. As diplomats, scholars, educators, journalists, politicians, and the public, it is essential to recognize the significance of the General Assembly in advancing global cooperation and achieving a more peaceful and sustainable world.

UN Agencies and Programs: Promoting Cooperation Across Borders

In an increasingly interconnected world, the importance of international cooperation and diplomacy cannot be understated. The United Nations (UN) plays a crucial role in promoting collaboration and addressing global challenges through its numerous agencies and programs. This subchapter explores the ways in which the UN facilitates cooperation across borders to achieve common goals.

One of the primary functions of the UN is to foster peace and stability through its peacekeeping missions. These missions have been deployed to conflict zones around the world, providing a platform for dialogue and negotiation, and helping to resolve disputes peacefully. The impact of these missions cannot be underestimated, as they have saved countless lives and facilitated post-conflict reconstruction.

The UN has also been at the forefront of promoting gender equality and women's empowerment. Through programs such as UN Women, the organization is working to eliminate gender-based discrimination and violence, increase women's participation in decision-making processes, and ensure equal access to education and economic opportunities. These efforts are crucial for achieving sustainable development and creating a more equitable world.

Furthermore, the UN recognizes the importance of addressing global health challenges. Through agencies like the World Health Organization (WHO), the UN works to combat diseases, improve healthcare systems, and promote universal access to essential medicines. The recent COVID-19 pandemic has highlighted the critical role of the UN in coordinating global efforts to control the spread of the virus and ensure equitable access to vaccines.

Climate change and environmental sustainability are pressing issues that require international cooperation. The UN's initiatives, such as the Paris Agreement, aim to limit global warming and promote sustainable development. Through programs like the United Nations Environment Programme (UNEP), the organization works to mobilize governments, businesses, and civil society to take action against climate change, protect biodiversity, and promote sustainable resource management.

In the realm of international development and poverty reduction, the UN plays a crucial role. Through agencies like the United Nations Development Programme (UNDP), the organization works to eradicate poverty, promote inclusive economic growth, and ensure access to basic services such as education, healthcare, and clean water. The UN's efforts have led to significant progress in reducing poverty and improving living conditions in many parts of the world.

Human rights and global justice are fundamental principles that the UN upholds. Through the Office of the High Commissioner for Human Rights (OHCHR), the organization monitors human rights violations, advocates for justice, and supports the establishment of international tribunals. The UN's commitment to human rights is essential in ensuring the protection and dignity of all individuals, regardless of their nationality or background.

In times of humanitarian crises and natural disasters, the UN is often at the forefront of providing aid and relief. Through agencies like the United Nations Children's Fund (UNICEF) and the World Food Programme (WFP), the organization delivers life-saving assistance, including food, water, shelter, and healthcare, to those in need. The UN's rapid response and coordination efforts are crucial for saving lives and alleviating suffering.

Education and literacy are vital for human development and empowerment. The UN's initiatives, such as the United Nations Educational, Scientific and Cultural Organization (UNESCO), work to promote access to quality education, eradicate illiteracy, and foster cultural dialogue. These efforts are instrumental in building inclusive societies and fostering global understanding.

Lastly, the UN plays a pivotal role in promoting international cooperation and diplomacy. Through its General Assembly, Security Council, and other specialized agencies, the organization provides a platform for dialogue, negotiation, and consensus-building among member states. The UN's commitment to multilateralism ensures that global challenges are addressed collectively, with the aim of finding shared solutions.

In conclusion, the UN's agencies and programs are instrumental in promoting cooperation across borders. Whether it is peacekeeping missions, gender equality, global health, climate change, international development, human rights, humanitarian aid, education, or diplomacy, the UN plays a vital role in addressing global challenges and achieving common goals. Despite its imperfections, the UN continues to be a driving force for positive change in the world, bringing together diplomats, scholars, educators, journalists, politicians, and the public in pursuit of a more peaceful, just, and sustainable future.

United Nations' Efforts in Resolving Disputes through Mediation and Negotiation

The United Nations (UN) has played a crucial role in resolving disputes through mediation and negotiation, contributing to global peace and security. This subchapter explores the UN's significant efforts in this area, highlighting its successes and imperfections.

Mediation and negotiation have been at the core of the UN's conflict resolution efforts since its establishment in 1945. The UN Charter grants the organization the authority to intervene in conflicts and promote peaceful settlements. Through its various bodies such as the Security Council and the Department of Political Affairs, the UN has been actively engaged in resolving disputes worldwide.

One of the key successes of the UN in this regard is its mediation efforts in ending conflicts and preventing their escalation. The peacekeeping missions conducted by the UN have been instrumental in facilitating negotiations and bringing conflicting parties to the table. For instance, the successful mediation in the Iran-Iraq conflict in the 1980s highlights the UN's ability to mediate in even the most complex disputes.

Moreover, the UN has made significant progress in developing frameworks and guidelines for effective mediation and negotiation. The Department of Political Affairs has been actively involved in training mediators and facilitating dialogue processes. These efforts have helped build local capacities and fostered sustainable peace in many post-conflict societies.

However, the UN's mediation and negotiation efforts are not without challenges and limitations. The organization's lack of enforcement mechanisms and the veto power of the Security Council's permanent members often hinder progress. Additionally, the UN's reliance on member states' political will and the complex nature of conflicts make successful mediation a daunting task.

Despite these challenges, the UN's commitment to resolving disputes through peaceful means remains steadfast. The organization continues to deploy mediators and peacekeepers to conflict zones, working tirelessly to promote dialogue, reconciliation, and peacebuilding. The UN's involvement in conflict resolution not only saves lives but also contributes to the overall stability and development of nations.

In conclusion, the UN's efforts in resolving disputes through mediation and negotiation have been commendable. While there are challenges and imperfections, the organization's successes in preventing and ending conflicts cannot be overlooked. As diplomats, scholars, educators, journalists, politicians, and the public, we must acknowledge and support the UN's role in promoting peaceful settlements, as it is essential for a more secure and prosperous world.

The United Nations' Contributions to International Peace and Security

The United Nations (UN) has played a crucial role in promoting international peace and security since its establishment in 1945. With the primary objective of preventing wars and maintaining peaceful coexistence among nations, the UN has made significant contributions in this field.

One of the major achievements of the UN is its peacekeeping missions. These missions have been deployed to conflict zones around the world, providing stability and security to war-torn regions. Through the deployment of peacekeepers, the UN has successfully prevented the escalation of conflicts, facilitated the disarmament of combatants, and protected civilians in volatile situations. These efforts have not only saved countless lives but also created an environment for peace negotiations and long-term stability.

In addition to peacekeeping, the UN has put substantial efforts into promoting gender equality and women's empowerment. Recognizing the crucial role that women play in peacebuilding and conflict resolution, the UN has actively worked towards increasing their participation in decision-making processes. Through initiatives such as the Women, Peace, and Security agenda, the UN has advocated for the inclusion of women in peace negotiations, post-conflict reconstruction, and peacebuilding efforts. This has not only empowered women but also contributed to the overall effectiveness and sustainability of peace processes.

The UN has also played a significant role in addressing global health challenges. With initiatives like the World Health Organization (WHO), the UN has worked towards ensuring access to affordable and quality healthcare for all. The UN has played a pivotal role in combating deadly diseases such as HIV/AIDS, malaria, and Ebola, providing essential medical supplies, expertise, and support to affected regions. By coordinating international efforts, the UN has been instrumental in preventing and controlling pandemics, saving millions of lives in the process.

Furthermore, the UN has been at the forefront of combating climate change and promoting environmental sustainability. Through agreements like the Paris Agreement, the UN has brought together nations to collectively address the urgent threat of climate change. By facilitating dialogue, setting targets, and promoting sustainable practices, the UN has been instrumental in raising awareness and driving action to protect the planet for future generations.

The UN's contributions to international development and poverty reduction cannot be overstated. Through programs like the Millennium Development Goals (MDGs) and the current Sustainable Development Goals (SDGs), the UN has mobilized global efforts to eradicate extreme poverty, promote education, improve health outcomes, and achieve sustainable economic growth. By providing funding, technical assistance, and policy guidance, the UN has helped countries make significant progress in these areas, lifting millions out of poverty and improving their quality of life.

Moreover, the UN has been a strong advocate for human rights and global justice. Through the Universal Declaration of Human Rights and various international treaties, the UN has set standards and norms to protect and promote human rights worldwide. By monitoring and reporting on human rights violations, the UN has shed light on atrocities and worked towards ensuring accountability and justice.

Additionally, the UN has been actively involved in humanitarian aid and disaster relief efforts. Through agencies like the United Nations High Commissioner for Refugees (UNHCR) and the World Food Programme (WFP), the UN has provided life-saving assistance to millions of people affected by natural disasters, conflicts, and displacement. By coordinating international responses and providing essential resources, the UN has helped alleviate suffering and restore hope in some of the most challenging circumstances.

Furthermore, the UN has recognized the pivotal role of education and literacy in achieving sustainable development. Through initiatives like Education for All and the Global Education First Initiative, the UN has promoted access to quality education for all, emphasizing the importance of lifelong learning and skills development. By advocating for inclusive and equitable education systems, the UN has empowered individuals and communities, enabling them to reach their full potential.

The UN has also played a crucial role in promoting international cooperation and diplomacy. Through its platforms for dialogue and negotiation, such as the General Assembly and the Security Council, the UN has facilitated discussions and resolutions on critical global issues. By bringing together diplomats, scholars, educators, journalists, politicians, and the public, the UN has fostered a culture of dialogue and understanding, promoting peaceful resolutions to conflicts and addressing shared challenges.

Lastly, the UN has taken the lead in promoting the Sustainable Development Goals (SDGs). These goals provide a comprehensive framework for addressing global challenges, including poverty, inequality, climate change, and sustainable development. By rallying nations and stakeholders around these goals, the UN has mobilized collective action and resources to create a more just, inclusive, and sustainable world.

In conclusion, the United Nations has made significant contributions to international peace and security. Through peacekeeping missions, efforts to promote gender equality, initiatives to address global health challenges, actions to combat climate change, and advancements in various other fields, the UN has played a crucial role in improving the lives of people worldwide. While the organization is not without imperfections, its successes demonstrate the importance and potential of international cooperation in addressing global challenges and promoting a more peaceful and prosperous world.

Chapter 11: United Nations' Initiatives in Promoting Sustainable Development Goals (SDGs)

The Sustainable Development Goals: A Blueprint for a Better Future

The Sustainable Development Goals (SDGs) represent a transformative agenda that aims to address the most pressing global challenges of our time. In this subchapter, we will explore how the SDGs serve as a blueprint for a better future, fostering international cooperation and promoting sustainable development across various sectors.

The SDGs, adopted by all United Nations member states in 2015, consist of 17 interconnected goals that encompass a wide range of issues, including poverty eradication, quality education, gender equality, climate action, and sustainable cities. These goals provide a comprehensive framework for governments, organizations, and individuals to work towards a more equitable, prosperous, and environmentally sustainable world.

One of the key strengths of the SDGs lies in their universality. Unlike their predecessor, the Millennium Development Goals, the SDGs apply to all countries, recognizing that sustainable development is a shared responsibility. This inclusivity encourages collaboration and knowledge sharing among nations, fostering a sense of global solidarity.

The SDGs have already made significant strides in addressing global challenges. United Nations peacekeeping missions have played a crucial role in maintaining peace and stability in conflict-affected regions, contributing to the achievement of Goal 16: Peace, Justice, and Strong Institutions. These missions have helped to prevent conflicts, protect civilians, and facilitate post-conflict reconstruction, creating an environment conducive to sustainable development.

Another area where the United Nations has made significant progress is in promoting gender equality and women's empowerment, in line with Goal 5. The organization has championed initiatives such as the HeForShe campaign, which encourages men to stand up for gender equality. The United Nations Entity for Gender Equality and the Empowerment of Women (UN Women) has been instrumental in advocating for women's rights and supporting gender mainstreaming efforts globally.

The United Nations has also been at the forefront of addressing global health challenges, particularly through the World Health Organization (WHO). The WHO has led efforts to combat infectious diseases, promote universal health coverage, and strengthen health systems, contributing to the achievement of Goal 3: Good Health and Well-Being.

In the face of climate change and environmental degradation, the United Nations has spearheaded initiatives to promote sustainable development and combat climate change, in line with Goal 13: Climate Action. The Paris Agreement, adopted under the auspices of the United Nations Framework Convention on Climate Change (UNFCCC), represents a landmark achievement in international efforts to mitigate greenhouse gas emissions and adapt to the impacts of climate change.

The United Nations' contribution to international development and poverty reduction cannot be overstated. Through initiatives such as the Millennium Development Goals and the Sustainable Development Goals, the organization has mobilized resources, promoted inclusive economic growth, and supported poverty eradication efforts worldwide.

The promotion of human rights and global justice is another core pillar of the United Nations' work. The organization has been instrumental in establishing international human rights standards, monitoring compliance, and advocating for the rights of marginalized groups. The United Nations Human Rights Council and the Office of the High Commissioner for Human Rights play a crucial role in upholding human rights globally.

In times of humanitarian crises and natural disasters, the United Nations has been a vital source of support. Through its specialized agencies, such as the United Nations High Commissioner for Refugees (UNHCR) and the United Nations Children's Fund (UNICEF), the organization provides life-saving assistance, protection, and advocacy for those in need.

Education and literacy are fundamental human rights and crucial drivers of sustainable development. The United Nations Educational, Scientific and Cultural Organization (UNESCO) leads efforts to promote quality education for all, aligning with Goal 4: Quality Education. The organization works towards improving access to education, enhancing the quality of learning, and fostering global citizenship.

International cooperation and diplomacy lie at the heart of the United Nations' mandate. The organization serves as a platform for dialogue, negotiation, and consensus-building among nations, promoting peaceful resolutions to conflicts and addressing shared challenges. The United Nations' role in promoting international cooperation and diplomacy is essential for achieving the SDGs.

In conclusion, the Sustainable Development Goals serve as a comprehensive blueprint for a better future. The United Nations plays a vital role in promoting and implementing these goals, fostering international cooperation, and addressing global challenges. By working together, governments, organizations, and individuals can create a more equitable, sustainable, and prosperous world for all.

United Nations' Efforts in Implementing and Monitoring the SDGs

The United Nations has been at the forefront of global development efforts, working tirelessly to address the world's most pressing challenges. One of its most significant initiatives is the implementation and monitoring of the Sustainable Development Goals (SDGs). These 17 goals, adopted in 2015, aim to end poverty, protect the planet, and ensure prosperity for all by 2030.

The United Nations plays a crucial role in driving the implementation of the SDGs. Through its various specialized agencies, programs, and funds, it mobilizes resources, coordinates actions, and supports member states in their efforts to achieve the goals. The UN's extensive network and partnerships enable it to bring together governments, civil society organizations, and the private sector to work towards a common vision.

Monitoring progress is a crucial aspect of the SDGs, and the United Nations takes this responsibility seriously. The UN's statistical system collects data on various indicators related to the goals, providing valuable insights into the progress being made and the areas that require more attention. This data is essential for evidence-based decision-making and resource allocation, ensuring that efforts are targeted where they are most needed.

The United Nations also promotes accountability and transparency in the implementation of the SDGs. It encourages member states to report on their progress and challenges through voluntary national reviews, which facilitate peer learning and exchange of best practices. Additionally, the UN supports the establishment of national mechanisms to monitor and review progress, ensuring that governments are held accountable for their commitments.

Furthermore, the UN fosters international cooperation and partnerships to accelerate progress towards the SDGs. It facilitates knowledge sharing, capacity building, and technology transfer among countries, enabling them to learn from each other's experiences and leverage resources more effectively. The UN's convening power brings together diverse stakeholders to collectively address common challenges and find innovative solutions.

While progress has been made in implementing the SDGs, challenges remain. The COVID-19 pandemic has further exacerbated existing inequalities and hampered progress towards the goals. However, the United Nations is committed to staying the course and redoubling its efforts. It continues to advocate for increased financing, policy coherence, and transformative actions to ensure that no one is left behind.

In conclusion, the United Nations' efforts in implementing and monitoring the SDGs are crucial for achieving sustainable development worldwide. By mobilizing resources, fostering partnerships, and promoting accountability, the UN plays a central role in driving progress towards the goals. As diplomats, scholars, educators, journalists, politicians, and the public, we must support and actively engage with the UN's endeavors to build a more prosperous, equitable, and sustainable world for future generations.

The Role of Member States in Achieving the SDGs

The Sustainable Development Goals (SDGs) are a set of 17 goals established by the United Nations (UN) to address the world's most pressing social, economic, and environmental challenges by the year 2030. While the UN plays a crucial role in coordinating and promoting these goals, the ultimate responsibility for their achievement lies with the member states. This subchapter will explore the important role that member states play in achieving the SDGs.

Member states are at the forefront of implementing the SDGs within their own countries. They are responsible for translating the global goals into national policies and strategies that are tailored to their specific contexts. This requires strong political will and leadership to prioritize the SDGs and integrate them into national development plans. Member states must also allocate adequate resources and establish effective monitoring and evaluation mechanisms to track progress towards the goals.

In addition to implementing the SDGs domestically, member states also have a role to play in advancing the goals globally. This includes engaging in international cooperation and diplomacy to address cross-border challenges such as climate change, poverty, and inequality. Member states must work together to share knowledge, best practices, and innovative solutions to accelerate progress towards the SDGs. They should also collaborate with international organizations, civil society, and the private sector to leverage resources and expertise.

Furthermore, member states have a responsibility to report on their progress towards the SDGs through voluntary national reviews (VNRs). These reviews provide a platform for member states to share their experiences, successes, and challenges in implementing the goals. They also facilitate mutual learning and peer-to-peer exchange, allowing member states to inspire and support each other in achieving the SDGs.

While the UN provides a framework and platform for member states to work towards the SDGs, it is ultimately the commitment and action of member states that will determine the success of these global goals. Therefore, it is crucial for member states to prioritize the SDGs, integrate them into their national agendas, and work collaboratively at the international level to achieve a sustainable and prosperous future for all.

In conclusion, member states play a pivotal role in achieving the SDGs. They are responsible for implementing the goals domestically, advancing them globally through cooperation and diplomacy, and reporting on their progress through VNRs. The commitment and action of member states are essential for the success of the SDGs, and it is through their collective efforts that we can build a more sustainable and equitable world.

Partnerships for Sustainable Development: Collaboration with Civil Society and Private Sector

In the pursuit of achieving the Sustainable Development Goals (SDGs), the United Nations recognizes the importance of collaboration with civil society and the private sector. This subchapter explores the vital role that partnerships play in driving sustainable development and the efforts undertaken by the UN to foster collaboration with these stakeholders.

Civil society organizations (CSOs) and the private sector bring unique perspectives, resources, and expertise to the table. Their involvement is crucial for creating innovative solutions and implementing effective strategies to address the complex challenges faced by societies worldwide.

The UN has actively engaged with civil society organizations, including non-governmental organizations (NGOs) and community-based groups, to promote inclusive and participatory approaches to development. By providing platforms for dialogue and consultation, the UN has facilitated the meaningful engagement of civil society in decision-making processes. These partnerships have resulted in the successful implementation of numerous development projects, particularly at the grassroots level.

Similarly, the private sector has emerged as a key partner in advancing the SDGs. Through corporate social responsibility initiatives, businesses have contributed to poverty reduction, environmental conservation, and social empowerment. The UN has worked to foster stronger partnerships with the private sector, encouraging responsible business practices and leveraging the resources and technological advancements that the corporate world brings to the table.

Partnerships with civil society and the private sector have been instrumental in achieving key milestones in sustainable development. For instance, collaborations between the UN and CSOs have led to significant advancements in promoting gender equality and women's empowerment. Through joint efforts, initiatives such as the inclusion of women in decision-making processes, the elimination of gender-based violence, and the promotion of equal access to education and healthcare have gained momentum.

Likewise, partnerships with the private sector have facilitated breakthroughs in addressing global health challenges, such as the eradication of diseases, the improvement of healthcare infrastructure, and the development of life-saving technologies. These collaborations have also played a crucial role in advancing environmental sustainability, with joint efforts leading to innovative solutions for combating climate change, promoting renewable energy, and preserving biodiversity.

The UN recognizes that achieving sustainable development requires the collective efforts of all stakeholders. Through partnerships with civil society and the private sector, the organization has been able to harness the expertise and resources required to drive progress towards the SDGs. By fostering collaboration and inclusivity, the UN continues to celebrate the successes of these imperfect partnerships, acknowledging that sustainable development is a shared responsibility that requires the active participation of all.

Overcoming Challenges and Ensuring the Success of the SDGs

The Sustainable Development Goals (SDGs) have emerged as a comprehensive framework to address the world's most pressing challenges, ranging from poverty and hunger to climate change and gender inequality. However, achieving these goals requires concerted efforts and overcoming various challenges. In this subchapter, we will explore the challenges faced in implementing the SDGs and discuss strategies to ensure their success.

One of the key challenges in implementing the SDGs is the lack of political will and commitment from member states. While the goals are universally accepted, translating them into concrete actions requires strong leadership and dedication. Diplomats and politicians must prioritize the SDGs in their policy-making processes and allocate resources accordingly. Furthermore, effective governance and institutional frameworks are essential to ensure accountability and transparency in the implementation of SDGs.

Another challenge is the complexity and interconnectivity of the goals themselves. The SDGs are interconnected and mutually reinforcing, meaning progress in one goal often depends on progress in others. This requires a comprehensive and integrated approach to development, which can be challenging to achieve. Scholars and educators play a critical role in promoting interdisciplinary research and education to enhance understanding of the interdependencies between the goals and their potential synergies.

Journalists have a crucial role to play in raising awareness about the SDGs and holding governments accountable for their commitments. By reporting on progress, challenges, and success stories related to the SDGs, journalists can contribute to public discourse and mobilize public support for the goals.

One of the most significant challenges to achieving the SDGs is financing. The goals require substantial financial resources, and mobilizing these resources remains a significant hurdle. Politicians and policymakers must explore innovative funding mechanisms, such as public-private partnerships and impact investments, to bridge the financing gap. The public can also play a role by advocating for increased funding for the SDGs and holding governments accountable for their financial commitments.

In conclusion, the SDGs represent a transformative agenda for global development. To ensure their success, diplomats, scholars, educators, journalists, politicians, and the public must collectively overcome challenges such as political will, interconnectivity, financing, and awareness. By working together and leveraging their respective roles, these stakeholders can contribute to the achievement of the SDGs and create a more sustainable and equitable world.

Conclusion: Reflecting on the United

Conclusion: Reflecting on the United Nations: Celebrating Successes and Imperfections

The United Nations has undoubtedly made significant strides in tackling global challenges and promoting cooperation among nations. As we conclude our exploration of the United Nations' successes and imperfections, it is crucial to reflect on the organization's achievements in various spheres, including peacekeeping missions, gender equality, global health, climate change, international development, human rights, humanitarian aid, education, and sustainable development goals.

One of the most notable accomplishments of the United Nations has been its peacekeeping missions. These missions have played a pivotal role in preventing and resolving conflicts, saving countless lives, and facilitating the transition to stability and peace in war-torn regions. The United Nations' commitment to maintaining peace has been instrumental in fostering a more secure and prosperous world.

Moreover, the United Nations has made commendable efforts in promoting gender equality and women's empowerment. By advocating for women's rights, providing support to women's organizations, and implementing policies that ensure equal opportunities, the United Nations has contributed to the advancement of gender equality globally.

The organization has also played a vital role in addressing global health challenges. Through initiatives such as the World Health Organization, the United Nations has coordinated efforts to combat diseases, enhance healthcare systems, and improve access to essential medicines. These endeavors have undoubtedly saved lives and improved the well-being of communities worldwide.

In tackling climate change and environmental sustainability, the United Nations has been at the forefront of international cooperation. Through agreements such as the Paris Agreement, the organization has mobilized nations to reduce greenhouse gas emissions, promote renewable energy, and protect our planet for future generations.

Furthermore, the United Nations has been instrumental in international development and poverty reduction. Through programs such as the Millennium Development Goals and now the Sustainable Development Goals, the organization has worked tirelessly to eradicate poverty, improve access to education and healthcare, and promote sustainable economic growth in developing countries.

The United Nations' commitment to human rights and global justice is another area where it has made a significant impact. By advocating for the protection and promotion of human rights, the organization has helped create a more just and equitable world.

In times of humanitarian crises and natural disasters, the United Nations has been at the forefront of providing aid and relief to affected communities. Their swift response and coordination efforts have saved lives and provided vital support to those in need.

The United Nations has also recognized the importance of education and literacy in fostering sustainable development and empowering individuals. Through initiatives such as the Global Education First Initiative, the organization has worked towards ensuring quality education for all, regardless of their socio-economic background.

Lastly, the United Nations' role in promoting international cooperation and diplomacy cannot be overstated. By providing a platform for dialogue and negotiation, the organization has fostered understanding and collaboration among nations, ultimately contributing to global peace and stability.

In conclusion, while the United Nations is not without its imperfections, its successes in various areas are undeniable. The organization's commitment to peacekeeping, gender equality, global health, climate change, international development, human rights, humanitarian aid, education, and sustainable development goals have had a profound impact on the world. As diplomats, scholars, educators, journalists, politicians, and the public, it is essential for us to celebrate these successes while recognizing the need for continuous improvement and reform within the United Nations. Together, we can work towards a more prosperous, just, and sustainable future for all.